OUR LADY OF
PERPETUAL SORROW

Willow River Press is an imprint of Between the Lines Publishing. The Willow River Press name and logo are trademarks of Between the Lines Publishing.

Copyright © 2023 by Terri Campion

Cover design by Cherie Fox

Between the Lines Publishing
1769 Lexington Ave N, Ste 286
Roseville MN 55113
btwnthelines.com

First Published: April 2024

ISBN: (Paperback) 978-1-958901-70-0

ISBN: (eBook) 978-1-958901-71-7

OUR LADY OF
PERPETUAL SORROW

Terri Campion

Early reviews for *Our Lady of Perpetual Sorrow*

"*Our Lady of Perpetual Sorrow* by Terri Campion is an original and delightful novel that blends both -comedy and the perpetual sorrow as foretold in the title. It is a tale of growing up in America in the 1960's. Campion shows the wonder and absurdity of the life of daughters, mothers, nuns and a whole cast of compelling characters. Much has been written about growing up Catholic, but Campion has added a fresh and poignant addition to the canon." **- Patty Dann, author of the *Mermaids; Starfish***

"*Our Lady of Perpetual Sorrow* is a vivid coming-of-age tale that is both hilarious and heartbreaking in equal measures. The book is narrated with searing honesty by Cassie, an inquisitive grade schooler trying to unravel the mysteries of Catholic doctrine, family relationships and her own confusing growth into womanhood. This well-crafted novel-in-stories resonates deeply with universal themes about growing up and finding one's place in the world." **- Lu Anne Stewart, author of the novel *Digging***

"*Our Lady of Perpetual Sorrow* is an interesting and original look on what it is like to be brought up as a Catholic child and grow into a Catholic adult. This new take on the religion will fascinate and delight both Catholics and whoever enjoys a good and witty read." **- Sara Banjeri, author of thirteen acclaimed novels including - *Shining Hero; Cobwebwalking***

For Karen

For Karen

Who Art in Heaven?

Where did the public-school kids go when they died? Did they have their own special afterworld? If so, where was it in relation to heaven? In a lower part of the sky? And, how was it decided who was born public and who was born Catholic?

It was on my way to school, my very first day, when I saw them – a swarm of kids of all shapes and sizes crossing our path and heading in every direction. There was no pattern or theme to their dress or movement, just a clash of plaids, stripes, khaki, and denim. Few carried book bags or anything schoolish like my siblings and I, who were lugging serious-looking leather satchels that were thin and floppy with their meager contents – a composition book and pencil case with two sharpened pencils. At the end of the day the bags would be heavy and bloated with hard covered textbooks.

My older sister and brother, and I, were walking up our street, on our way to Our Lady of Perpetual Sorrow's grade school with my mother, who was pushing our baby brother Freddy in a stroller.

"Where are they going?" I asked my sister Patty, who was instructed not to let go of my hand until we reached the school.

1

"They're public-school kids!" she shouted into my face. "They go to the public school!" She was entering the fourth grade, yet we were dressed identically, in a navy wool jumper over a crisp long-sleeved white blouse with a Peter Pan collar onto which was snapped a navy-blue bow tie. A navy-blue beanie sat atop our heads, held on with bobby pins, and our hair had been set and styled – by our mother – into short tidy flips that encircled our necks.

Our brother Greg, who was entering the sixth grade and not happy to be walking with this entourage, was wearing, a starched white long-sleeved shirt, navy tie, and navy slacks. All three of us were wearing black and white saddle shoes, freshly polished with new laces that I was already growing out of. I envied my mother and Freddy, who were dressed sensibly for this scorching day in shorts and sandals.

There was a procession of other children heading up our street, uniformed as we were, some with a parent, others in twos or small quiet groups. We seemed to be walking at a matching pace against the wave of rowdy children that surged through and around us like a tornado. My mother had prepared for this storm, arranging us into a moving fortress, walking four abreast, she the strong center with her height and full red lips – the stroller a toddler turret with Freddy, who was screeching in delight at the plethora of activity surrounding him.

When we turned right onto Beechnut Street, Patty was sucked into a swirl of girls and lost hold of my hand. My mother brought the caravan to a halt, wrapped my fingers around the stroller bar, yanked my sister out of the vortex, linked our hands back together, and resumed our journey.

"What did I tell you?" she barked at my sister.

"Cassie didn't hold on tight enough!" Patty met my pissed off puss with a wink, letting me know that she knew she was lying and would fix it later. My sister should have come with instructions. She wreaked havoc and intrigue everywhere she went and on everything and everyone that came in contact with her. The only person with immunity was our older brother, who had my back that day.

"Liar! I saw that! Mom she just winked at Cassie!"

"I did not!"

"You're such a liar!"

"Knock it off the two of you or, ELSE." The 'Else' meant different things to each of us – a spanking, confinement to your room, a guilt-ridden lecture by our father – it was enough to shut us up.

We were coming up to Our Lady of Perpetual Sorrow's block on Jackson Avenue. The wave of motley kids had ebbed into a trickle and the orderly uniformed children silently dominated the street. We passed the convent where a group of nuns were coming out the side door, their heads bowed, hands loosely folded in prayer below their collar. Suddenly a wave of grief washed over me. There would be no joy at this school. One of those serious sad sisters could be my teacher.

I looked around at the other Catholic kids as a bottle neck formed at the entrance to the schoolyard. There were no expressions of any kind on their faces. I wanted to turn around and join that gang of public-school kids who looked like they were coming from a party and going to a carnival. They were having fun on their way to school! We Catholic kids looked like we were going to a funeral or our own execution.

"Why can't I go to public school?" I yelled across my sister to my mother.

"Because you're Catholic," my mother muttered in a low breath, that I could still hear through the noise.

"But why? Why am I Catholic?" I insisted as the crowd came to a crawl.

"Because you were born Catholic."

I looked up at Patty and Greg for a show of solidarity, but there was no sign of life, let alone spunk in their eyes. They each had a blank zombie stare on their face. It was as if their batteries had been removed and the only evidence of life left behind were the beads of sweat lining their eyebrows and upper lips.

My mother rolled the stroller into the playground where lines of navy-blue clad children stood silently as several nuns and a few lay teachers with stern faces walked around and through the rows, patrolling. My brother and sister joined their respective lines while my mother and I stood off to the side along the fence with other mothers with toddlers and baby carriages. Except for Freddy's babbles it was eerily quiet considering there must have been a thousand bodies standing in the cement enclosure. The silence was soon broken when a square-shaped nun emerged from the school door ringing a handbell with gusto. At once and in unison, the lines of kids dropped to their knees and folded their hands in prayer.

"Cassie!" Freddy was reaching up to me in terror. My mother pulled him out of the stroller. He was three, verbal, ambulatory, and at that moment ready to run and so was I. I grabbed his hand but as I turned to go, my mother blocked me with her foot as she placed her attention on the square nun with the bell, walking towards us.

"Good morning, Mother."

"Hello Betty. And who do we have here? Are you ready for school young man?"

The nun's words didn't match her face, which was kind and smiling. Why was she addressing Freddy and not me? It was obvious that he was not ready for school. I was the one sweating under a navy wool jumper, in shoes that were torturing my feet. My brother was wearing a onesie.

As if she could read my mind even with her back to me, she turned around and said with a stern smile, "And you must be Catherine."

It wasn't really a question, so I didn't know whether to talk or not. Freddy was pulling on my hand. He needed to get out of there, and if that wasn't possible, I knew he would scream until it was.

"Yes, she is Mother. Catherine, aren't you going to answer Mother?"

Why was my mother calling this nun Mother? What was the question I was supposed to answer? I was failing first grade before I even stepped into the building. I kept my face on Freddy as I lifted my eyes to the nun's bosom and answered, "Yes?"

"She looks just like you, Betty."

I couldn't help but smile. My mother was pretty.

"Now that's much better. What a beautiful smile!" The nun had taken a step back and was eyeing me from head to toe as if she were searching for something else to compliment.

"She looks much better when she smiles, I keep telling her."

Now how was I supposed to keep this stupid grin on my face after that remark? My mother saw my face collapse and raised her eyebrows and gave her – 'what did I just say?' – kind of look to this nun, who responded with a nod, absently, as she produced a pocket watch with her free hand from the sheaths of black nylon, flipped it open, looked at it, snapped it shut, and slipped it back into the depths of her habit.

"Well then," she announced to us, "it's that time."

My mother stooped to my level, straightened my jumper, pushed my bangs out of my eyes, gave me a hug and a kiss then said, "You have a good day honey. Freddy, come give your sister a kiss goodbye."

No one had paid much attention to Freddy in the last thirty seconds and he was bubbling with grief, holding it all back, saving it for just the right moment, and this was it. He let out a blood-curdling wail as he clung to the bottom half of my jumper, "Nooo! Don't Go!"

Once my mother managed to extricate him from my uniform, the nun grabbed my hand, commanding: "You come with me, young lady." With her other hand, she began clanging the bell as the lines of students instantly, as one body, stood. Freddy's wails of protest continued as she pulled me into the school yard and dragged me across the playground past the lines of children, each line lower in height than the other until we got to the last line where the tiniest kids were standing next to the chain-link metal fence that separated the cement playground from the sidewalk. I could still hear Freddy's screams in my ears, but I wasn't sure if they were in real time, or an echo coming from inside me.

After nine months of afternoon kindergarten, I expected first grade to be an easy transition. I didn't have such a great time in kindergarten. It wasn't so much scary as stressful. There was this boy, Martin, who threw up a lot. He didn't give any warning. He could be talking to you or coloring and BLAH. There it was – throw-up everywhere. He didn't even try to make it to the bathroom. I felt a kind of dread throughout the day: Would he, or wouldn't he? It was hard to relax and learn things with the threat of a puddle of vomit hanging over your head. All summer I worried that he would be in my first-grade class and maybe even in every class for eight years!

Kindergarten was, for the most part, playtime and 'show and tell' with a nice, childless, middle-aged lady who loved children. We wore regular clothes and there were no tests or grades and no more than ten kids on any given day. Attendance wasn't mandatory and, fortunately, Martin was often absent.

There was nothing loosey-goosey about first grade. You had to show up every day at 8:30 in uniform, with an organized book bag, sharpened pencils and completed assignments. There were at least thirty-five kids in my class, luckily none of them were Martin. Our teacher was a young moody nun, with a smooth complexion and square nostrils. She seemed to be the happiest before lunch and at the end of the day. The cafeteria was a horror house of shouting and banging metal and smelled like used milk. Most of the other first graders seemed to be adapting well. There were a few criers, and kids that wet their pants and kids that puked, but even they calmed down after the first week. The others showed no hints of fear or rebellion, they just followed instructions. I did my best to not call attention to myself.

I was not a morning person. It took me forever to fall asleep at night. "Say a hundred 'Hail Marys!'" my father advised.

"What'll I do now?" I'd ask from the top of the stairs.

"Say a hundred more."

It didn't work. I was tired at the wrong time – 7:00 AM, when the wake-up attempts began in my house and the hour I would be in the deepest cycle of REM. My energy was at its peak twelve hours later at 7:30 PM, bedtime. My body never adjusted, and I would be sent to bed wide awake. To entertain myself I'd create movies in my mind where I was a prettier and more important person who didn't have to answer to anyone, or go to Catholic school, which made waking up to reality even more horrid.

Every day started and ended in prayers – verses of words I did not understand and were never explained. The Baltimore Catechism was the premiere textbook. It was filled with questions it answered itself, such as: "Who is God? God is the creator of heaven and earth and of all things." It offered no opportunity or consideration for questions a normal child might have, such as: "What exactly is a soul? Is it really like the circle Sister Marian would draw on the blackboard with every religion lesson, every day throughout first grade?

"This is a pure soul," Sister Marion would say and with a few back-and-forth strokes with the side of the chalk the circle became a full moon. "If you die with a pure soul, you will go straight to heaven."

"When you commit a venial sin, your soul will look like this." She'd then make tiny dark spots with the edge of the eraser on the white disk. "If you die with a venial sin on your soul, you will go to purgatory before going to heaven."

"And this is your soul when you commit a mortal sin." She would erase all the white out of the circle, then turn to us and ask, "Where does one go when they die with a mortal sin on their soul?" We were programmed to reply: "H. E.L.L." It was a venial sin to say the word.

I tried to imagine a one-dimensional disk stuck inside my ribcage, becoming marred with black spots whenever I committed a venial sin and the spots disappearing after I said, 'An Act of Contrition.' I wondered if you could feel the difference when it was pure or spotted. Did it feel heavier or cold when you committed a mortal sin? Did public school people have a soul? Or, was there something else inside their ribcage? There was no one to answer these questions. It was a concept I struggled to grasp on my own because it seemed I was the only one of my Catholic peers that looked confused whenever the topic came up. Were only nuns and priests allowed to talk about sins and souls? Did the rest of us just have to listen and not question what we were told? Life wasn't looking like much fun as a Catholic.

My cousin Gretchen and her two brothers, Kurt and Paul, were the first public school kids I knew. It didn't make sense to me at first because 'being born Catholic' meant to me that it was in our genetic make-up and anyone blood-related would also be 'born Catholic.'

"He gave it up when he married your Aunt Louise." My mother was talking about her brother, my Uncle George. I was in the process of becoming a real Catholic and would be receiving the sacrament of penance the following week. Every night around ten o'clock I'd go running down the stairs with another reason why I shouldn't become a 'real' Catholic. Instead of 'examining my conscience' like we were supposed to do before falling asleep, I was making last-ditch efforts to change my destination into becoming a non-denominational congregant. Someone open to all options, a wait-and-see kind of person who knew that at 'seven' she was not ready to commit to any one religion, especially one with so many strange and spooky rules and rituals.

"Won't he go to hell for doing that?" I asked. My parents were at the kitchen table. My mom was writing checks and stuffing them in envelopes.

"Probably," my dad said.

"Robert," my mother said in a scolding tone.

"If not that, something else will put him there." My dad took a sip of his beer, his eyes twinkling. My mother took a drag off her Kool and blew the smoke in his direction. My father swatted it back in her direction. Is this how they behaved when we kids weren't around?

"Go back to bed Cassie or you'll never be able to get up tomorrow," my mother said.

"I don't wanna get up tomorrow! I don't wanna make my Confession! It's not fair that my cousins don't hafta do it!" I said all this as I stomped with fury out of the kitchen, through the dining and living room and up the stairs, not caring who I woke up. Clearly, I had not reached the age of reason. Why couldn't they see that?

The next day was our first and only rehearsal for our confessional ceremony. Sister Michael Mary, the seventh-grade boys' teacher, and Sister George, the eighth-grade boys' teacher, acted as stand-ins for the priests. They each sat in a confessional box and went through the motions of the Confession – blessing, listening, reciting a prayer and doling out the penances. Sister Ann, a third-grade teacher and overseer of students crossing into Catholicism, was patrolling traffic, telling us where to go and when.

The church was dark and eerie even though it was a super sunny day and there were plenty of stained-glass windows on the east and west sides of the church for the sun to peer through. But it wasn't. My heart was thumping so hard and loud I was sure Christine Livingston who I was standing behind was going to turn around and tell me to "Cut it out!" Christine was my line partner in the walk from the school to the church. She was self-assured and well-groomed. I wondered if one had to do with the other. Sweat beads were forming on my upper lip and I was starting to feel chilled. And this was only the rehearsal! I would have to do this every week for the rest of my life! If I died now I'd definitely go to heaven. Maybe I could provoke somebody into killing me? Would these thoughts count as sins? My mind wouldn't shut up.

I was hoping that I would get Sister Michael Mary as my stand-in confessor, but it wasn't up to me. Sister Anne was parked between the two confessionals directing kids into the boxes with her boney hands that looked like they were sculpted from a block of ivory soap.

Christine lucked out and went into Michal Mary's box. I didn't know Sister Michael, but rumor was she was strict but fair. Sister George – how come these nuns had men's names? Was that why they were both teaching classes with all boys?

Oh no. It was happening. Before I could remember what the rumors were about Sister George, a pudgy blond boy with a scarlet face was trying to exit Sister George's box, but he kept getting caught in the purple velvet curtain. I looked over at Michael Mary's box hoping to see some movement – nothing. Sister Anne unraveled the blonde boy, shoved him along and was now holding the curtain and pointing at me.

My heartbeat was a motor that propelled me across the marble floor towards the confessional and Sister Anne, whose face up close looked illuminated from within. As if this moment could get any scarier.

I stepped behind the heavy velvet drape into a pitch-black space the size of a bathroom stall, stumbled onto a hard wooden plank and arranged myself into a kneeling position. With my hands folded on another wood plank, I waited for the cue to begin my Confession. After what could have been thirty seconds or thirty minutes, the panel three inches before my eyes slid open with a bang, revealing the profile of Sister George behind a latticed screen.

There was a bare light bulb on the ceiling of the booth that was so close to the top of her habit that if she tilted her head up straight, she could knock it out of the socket, or it could singe the black nylon and she would go up in flames. All this was going through my mind as I went through the routine that I had memorized and practiced so many times that the words meant nothing to me. I listed a few commandments I admitted to breaking and a random number of times I did so while she piously shook her head in disapproval, as if my phony transgressions were a personal affront.

In a deep smoky voice that could have passed for a man's, she gave me my penance: "Half of a rosary." She was taking this rehearsal too seriously.

When I got to the altar rail to say my penance, the pudgy blond boy was still there. He must have gotten a whole rosary. He was tapping his fingers in that way kids do when they're trying to keep count. He also looked like he had got caught in a lawn sprinkler on his way to the front of the church. I felt sorry for him. He was more scared than I was. I blessed myself and started my half rosary.

I was on the last Hail Mary of my first section when my best friend, Shelly Evans, who was in the other second grade class, knelt beside me and smiled. I hadn't seen a smile all morning. Before I could move my tight lips up into a return smile, she blessed herself and sprung off the altar rail, like she was stepping off a Ferris-wheel backwards. She was the second kid that had knelt beside me in the time I was up there. Michael Mary was giving mini penances!

These kids were coming out of her box – uplifted! I wanted to die, and pudgy kid looked like a yellow sponge after a cherry Kool-Aid spill. I was about to get really, really mad but then I realized – I was taking this too seriously! This was a rehearsal! The 'priest' and the 'sins' I confessed to were not real. Why should I accept the penance as real? I poked the pudgy kid in his cushy side. He turned to me with a candy red face and baby blue eyes blazing with terror.

"This is just a practice," I said in a loud whisper, "we don't have to say the whole penance."

He sucked in his lower lip as tears and snot began to pour down his pale moon face. I turned back to the altar and quickly blessed myself.

"Come on," I said in a normal voice, not caring who heard me, "you're forgiven." I stood up and waited as he blessed himself and lifted his bulky body off the altar rail.

The morning of the first Confession ceremony, I was awakened by the chirping of song sparrows and a gentle breeze fragrant with the aroma of the peonies and honey suckle from the bushes in the back yard. I opened my eyes to boughs of pink dogwood flowers against a cobalt blue sky. The universe was mocking me. This day called for foreboding weather with obstacles like lightening, high winds, and pelting hail. At the very least a cloudy cooler day befitting of a navy wool jumper and the other restrictive apparel we were required to wear.

The church was even darker than it had been on rehearsal day. It seemed bigger, or less crowded, I couldn't decide. I just wanted it to be tomorrow already, or this afternoon, or even an hour later. Sister Anne was at her post between the confessionals, looking like a statue, directing kids to either of the two boxes. It didn't matter to me which box I went into. I had only seen the priests of the parish from a distance, at the altar saying Mass, or strutting across the school yard to the church or rectory. Patty said the pastor of the parish was handsome but mean. Greg, who was an altar boy, told me about a younger priest who would over enunciate every word when he said Mass and if he mispronounced anything he would repeat it until he got it right. If I had to choose, I'd want the younger one – over enunciating was better than being mean.

As I knelt on the wooden plank waiting for the axe to come down on my neck, I heard a bit of chuckling from inside the box and then a cough. When the panel opened, I was met with a full-frontal smiling face that looked like Jethro from 'The Beverly Hillbillies', but older. I didn't know whether to start the confession or say "howdy!" After a second or two, he winked, nodded, and then turned his face to the side, which I took as my cue to begin.

At one point he started coughing or maybe he was chuckling, I couldn't tell. When I was finished, he turned full face and said, "Now that wasn't so bad was it? It'll get easier with time." He looked like he expected me to reply with normal conversation or leave, but I was not prepared to do either. 'What to do if the priest treats your Confession like a friendly visit' was not covered in our preparations for this sacrament. My stomach let loose a loud honk that sounded more like a release of gas than a cry of hunger. This was not going well.

"That yours or mine?" he asked.

"It was my stomach!" I knew he wasn't allowed by law to tell anyone about anything that happened in the confessional, including bodily emissions, but at that moment I felt that I could not go on living thinking this priest thought that sound was something other than it was.

"You didn't have breakfast?"

"Cheerios."

"Your most important meal."

"I know."

People were going to think I had a lot of sins to confess. As if he could hear my mind, he turned to the side, sashayed his forearm up and across, mumbling something like 'Our Father' and 'Hail Mary', then suddenly my booth was cast in darkness.

After experiencing the full-frontal smiling view of this priest and his concern for my stomach, then to be so abruptly dismissed, without a goodbye, I felt a little hurt. This religion had me on an emotional roller coaster before I was even completely indoctrinated. I quickly blessed myself, stood, grabbed the violet curtain at one end, shoved it aside, stepped out of the box and made my way to the altar rail, which was experiencing heavy turnover.

"You got Crackers!" Patty shrieked after I'd described the experience in detail, which was probably a sin in itself, but I didn't care as I was growing more skeptical with each step I took to becoming a true Catholic.

"I thought they had retired him," my mother said as she plopped a platter of pancakes in the middle of the table. The pancakes were my choice for a celebratory early lunch/late breakfast for making my first Confession.

"He still does confessions and weekday masses," Greg said. "His name is Craciolo."

"Crackers makes religion fun," Patty screeched.

"Quack Quack Quackers!" Freddy was rocking wildly in his booster chair. My mother nonchalantly caught him as he was about to fall and lifted him onto her lap.

"He drinks the altar wine and carries the chalice around with him like he's at a cocktail party!" Patty said, drizzling syrup over her one pancake in tiny circles.

"Who told you that?" Greg asked.

"You did," Patty said.

"No I didn't. Would you hurry up with that syrup!"

"Well, then maybe I saw him do it. I just know he does. Everybody knows it."

"Let the poor guy enjoy what's left of his life," my dad said as he slid another pancake onto his plate. "Where's the syrup?"

My mother grabbed the bottle out of Greg's hand as he was about to put it down on the table and set it in front of my father's plate.

"He's not that much older than you, Robert."

"Exactly," my father responded, as he poured a fountain of syrup onto his stack.

"I'm just glad it's over," I said.

"Over? It's just beginning."

Not sure who said that. But it was the truth, the goddamn truth.

The next week was filled with preparations for our first Holy Communion ceremony. It was a much more positive event, outright joyous compared to Confession. The traditional ceremony at Our Lady of Perpetual Sorrow was somewhat elaborate and required two rehearsals, with Sister George and Sister Michael standing in as the priests. There would be a procession around the four blocks that encompassed the parish led by the priests, and a posse of altar boys carrying a huge crucifix and canisters of smoking frankincense.

This was to be the first of many processions for me in the years to come at Our Lady of Perpetual Sorrow, and it was the most fun I'd had at the school to date. We walked in lines of two – shortest to tallest, girls separate from boys with our same partners from the Confession ceremony.

One of the best parts about the Communion ceremony was that the girls got to wear a beautiful white dress and veil of our own choosing, along with white shoes, anklets, and gloves. The store to go to for your Communion dress in Cloverdale was Belle's Baby Boutique – a clothing store for kids, not just babies. The Belle family opened the store during the Baby Boom and decided to keep the catchy name.

"She'll never be able to wear her sister's clothes. She's growing this way," my mother made a vertical gesture with her arms and hands. "Her sister is growing this way." She traced an hourglass in the air. "How'd that happen?"

Hazel Belle was wrapping up my Communion outfit – dress, white patent leather baby doll shoes, white socks, gloves, a lace veil with satin roses, and a blow-up petticoat which I was not happy about.

"I can't have them running around looking like rag dolls." My mother was taking money out of her wallet. "They'll just cost me a fortune until they're eighteen."

"Well Betty," Hazel Belle said as she handed my mother back a few bills, "I could use some help around here and in the Ladies Boutique."

"I'd love to!" my mother cried out.

"You'd get a twenty percent discount," Hazel continued.

"I'd really, really love to…work!" my mother sniffed as she daintily covered the bottom half of her face. Hazel came from behind the counter and took my mother into her arms and patted and rubbed her back saying things like "there, there," and "it's okay, you go ahead and have yourself a cry."

And that was the beginning of my mother's career in fashion retail.

When we met in our classroom before the procession, the girls were each given a nosegay with tiny pink and white roses, lilies, white carnations, and baby's breath wrapped in a white satin bow. This was one of the few times in grade school that I was glad to be a girl. The only thing special about the boy's outfit was the white tie. They didn't seem to care, but it did look as if they were paying more attention to the girls, and they seemed nicer. Most had their hair gelled and firmly parted.

Christine Livingston and I were the only girls with blow-up petticoats. Fearing that the two of us walking in tandem would form a bulge in the line and thus inspire chaos, Sister Anne put me a few spaces behind and partnered me with Linda Warner. I didn't mind, I was beginning to realize that Christine didn't have much of a sense of humor. She was acting all high and mighty with her puffy petticoat, whereas I was trying to deflate mine.

Besides, I had other things on my mind. It was this whole 'transubstantiation' thing with the bread and wine being transformed into the body and blood of Christ, then cut into millions of quarter-shaped discs and placed onto the tongues of billions of people around the world. I had no choice but to take part in this ritual and act like a believer. No one really knew what was going on in my head – except God.

After walking around the block, with scores of people lining the streets watching and waving to us, we filed into the church like a wedding ceremony, with our closest family members standing in the back pews and along the walls observing as we made our way to the front of the church and took our place in the front four pews. All three priests of the parish were on the altar with Father Tilman, the pastor and mean priest according to Patty, leading the mass. Greg was up there also, and I was hoping he wouldn't be the one to hold the gold plate under my chin.

When I sat down in the pew, the front part of my dress popped up.

17

When I pushed it down, the sides shot up. I spent the sitting part of the mass holding the dress down with my arms. Every time I stood or kneeled the skirt flew up around, hitting the girls on either side of me. Christine was in the pew in front of me, taking up space for three with her expansive petticoat, looking like a princess sitting on a throne.

Maybe trying to deflate this thing was a mistake. Walking to the altar the skirt was flopping up and down, left and right. I kept my focus on the back of Linda's head and tried to count the number of Bobby pins she used to keep her hair in place under her veil.

As I knelt at the altar rail the sides and back of the skirt flew up and around me. There was no controlling it. I was no longer embarrassed, I was amused. As long as I didn't make eye contact with anyone and kept my mind on the horrors of transubstantiation, I wouldn't break into a laughing fit.

Transubstantiation was a big word. Greg told me that word. Oh no. Where was he? If he saw me he wouldn't be able to control himself and would have to leave the altar, and with only two altar boys, the ceremony would run overtime.

Priests were approaching me from both sides. I was in the middle of the altar.

There was a point where the one would stop and go back to the other side. At least that was what the nuns did in the rehearsals. Today there were three priests so that system might not work so well. My eyes were on the marble floor on the other side of the altar rail. I was trying to picture Greg's feet and the shoes he was wearing when I felt a cold jab on my neck.

I lifted my chin and eyes to see Father Tilman holding 'the Body of Christ' in front of my face and mumbling a prayer. I opened my mouth and gently stuck out my tongue like we were trained to do as I received my first Holy Eucharist. The priest quickly blessed me and moved on to

Linda. Now that this part was over, I allowed myself a quick glance to see who was holding the gold plate that jabbed my neck. It was my brother.

My Uncle George, Aunt Louise, and my three Protestant cousins were sitting in our living room with Patty and Freddy when I arrived home from the church with my mother and father. They had been part of the outdoor audience. Kurt and Greg were the same age – twelve. Paul was five, Freddie four, and Gretchen eight, a year older than me.

"We beat you and we walked home!" Patty shouted as she sprung from the couch. "What happened to your dress?"

"Don't you look like a little bride!" Aunt Louise said.

"You want a beer, George?" my dad asked my uncle as he headed into the kitchen.

"Robert, it's not even noon," my mother scolded.

My uncle chuckled, "Ask me in another five minutes, Bob."

Gretchen was staring at my outfit. She had on a cute pink and green checkered short set. Her hair was brown like mine but straight and shiny. She didn't have any freckles and her eyes were the color of my birthstone – sapphire. I hated her. I started to go upstairs to get out of the ridiculous dress that was now bouncing in four directions at once.

"Young lady, where are you going?" my mother asked in her bossiest voice.

"Upstairs."

"Don't be smart. You're not changing out of that dress."

"Why not?"

"It's your own fault for letting the air out. You saw how lovely and ladylike Christine looked."

"Christine Livingston?" Patty asked with a screech. "She's so beautiful!"

Anybody who didn't have freckles and wasn't fat was beautiful to Patty, even nuns and older ladies.

"You said she was a snotty snob!" I wasn't going to let Patty get away with being a two-faced liar today.

"So? You ever see an ugly snotty snob?"

I wanted to tear her eyes out right then and there. Before I could do that, my mother took my hand and led me back into the room.

"Come show your aunt your petticoat."

"I wanna see it too!" Gretchen was touching every part of the dress while my aunt was inspecting the petticoat and the tube. My mother grabbed the nozzle and started blowing the damn thing back up.

"We're going to take some pictures," she said.
"Robert, get your camera.

20

The next half hour or so was spent lining up various assortments of people, me the main attraction, after the petticoat. Everyone had given me a 'religious' present. My aunt and uncle gave me a statue of the Infant of Prague, who I'd never heard of. Gretchen gave me a holy card with a picture of Christ nailed to the cross. Kurt gave me a miniature prayer book with silky pages and a picture of a girl with brown hair in a Communion outfit on the cover. I was really touched. They must have gone to a lot of trouble to find these Catholic accessories or whatever you called them.

"We shopped at that little store inside the church," Gretchen said.

Well, there went that theory.

"I didn't," Kurt said, "I got my present last week."

My heart skipped a beat. He went out of his way for me!

"Thank you," I said, making eye contact with him. I'd already thanked everyone, but I thought he deserved a second, more personal thank you.

At 12:30, the mothers set up the drinks for the ladies – white wine with club soda; the men – Schlitz Beer; the kids – a choice of orange juice, ginger ale or Tab.

"Now can I get out of this dress?"

"Yes, you can get out of the dress if you stop your whining."

"I'm not whining!" It was so embarrassing the way my mother treated me like a baby in front of my cousins. I started up the stairs.

"When's Greg getting home?" Kurt asked.

"He jabbed the gold plate in my neck!" I shouted from the third step. I hadn't told anyone about this. I ran back down and into the living room and was about to give details when Patty jumped up.

"He did that to me once and only once because you know what I did? And you should do this next time but do not tell him I told you to do it."

"Everybody knows about it, Patty," my dad said. He and my uncle were chuckling.

"I acted like I was choking, like this," Patty opened her mouth and widened her eyes dramatically. "Then I whispered: I'm choking! He never did it again."

"Who was the priest?" I asked.

"Father Tilman. Greg got in big trouble."

"I wish I could be an altar boy," Kurt said.

His father looked at him and scoffed, "No, you don't."

"Yes, I do!"

"You'd hate it, gettin' up at the crack of dawn every Sunday morning."

My uncle was standing in the middle of the living room, like he was on a stage. Kurt looked like he was ready to punch him.

"Just because you didn't like it –"

"All that Latin mumbo jumbo…"

My father was smiling, enjoying his brother-in-law's irreverence.

"That's all changing Dad. The whole mass's going to be in English."

My Uncle George pointed his index finger in his son's face. "How do you know about this?"

I felt a chill. I'd never seen this side of my uncle. It was as if I were watching my mother. That same cold meanness.

"I read!" Kurt left the room and went into the kitchen. I heard the back door shut.

I ran upstairs and quickly changed into a pale pink summer dress with red roses embroidered on the edges of the sleeves and collar. It was a compromise – I'd at least wear a dress today. I heard my brother's voice coming from the patio. I couldn't wait to relive that moment with him and have a good laugh together. But when I got downstairs, the two were gone. Greg hadn't even come into the house.

The gathering soon moved to the patio and backyard with the younger boys bopping from one activity to the other inside and outside – tinker toys, racing cars, Play-Doh. They didn't seem to agree or engage for any length of time on anything, but they were not giving up on each other. Patty, Gretchen, and I played hopscotch for a while.

Our dad had painted a permanent one on the patio in perfect and uniform proportions that only an engineer could muster. It took away the fun and creativity of making new ones with colored chalk, but we didn't tell him that. Our father was a Civil Engineer. I had no idea what that meant, and for the longest time I thought he was a polite train conductor. He and my uncle – who was an architect, and I knew what that was! – were setting up the outdoor grill while the ladies were in the kitchen preparing hamburger patties and salad.

Eventually we stopped playing and started helping our moms with bringing food, plates, and paper cups from the kitchen to the picnic table. There was something different about Gretchen that day. Usually, she and Patty were loud and showing off, trying to outshine each other. Even though there was a two-year difference in their ages, they were more compatible and interesting to each other than I was. I wished Kurt was a girl because he had a nice personality and didn't have to be the center of attention like his sister.

"What do you do about your sins?" I was opening and laying out the hamburger buns. Gretchen was doing the same with the hot dog buns.

"I don't know. What's a sin?"

"You don't know what a sin is?" How dumb was my cousin?

"Kinda. Don't get excited."

"It's when you do something bad. Or mean." I was hoping she'd see her behavior to me in that last part.

"I know that." Did she, or didn't she? She was trying to spin my head in circles, just like Patty.

"So what do you do to get rid of them? Catholics go to Confession and say prayers."

"Goody for the Catholics." Just like that she opened the last bun and walked away.

"You know you're lucky you don't have to wear a uniform and go to Mass!" She was out of ear shot. It was more than compatibility we lacked. We really didn't like each other.

Greg and Kurt walked into the backyard, sweaty, carrying a baseball bat and gloves, their pants splotched with dirt.

"Who won?" Uncle George asked.

"Nobody," Kurt answered.

"We were just playing," Greg said.

"Greg! That was so funny! I can't believe you did that!" I was bouncing around the yard like a Superball. I'd been looking forward to this moment all day.

"What'd I do?" he asked.

I was about to get really sad when Kurt said, "You choked her with the gold plate at her first Communion!"

"You jabbed it into my neck!" Now I was wishing Kurt wasn't my cousin so I could marry him some day. Greg was smiling.

"What was happening with that dress?"

"I was afraid to look at you because I thought you'd crack up!" My voice was gravelly and jumping octaves. I was having the time of my life talking to these older boys.

"Yea, me too."

"Well, well, well! If it isn't Wally and Butch." Our mother called from the kitchen window.

"Stop saying that!" Greg yelled.

24

"Who?" Kurt asked.

"The Little Rascals. I hate it when she calls me that."

"Go wash up!" Aunt Louise was coming through the back door balancing a drink and cigarette in one hand and a bowl of coleslaw in the other.

"Why do you hate that?" Kurt asked as they dropped their baseball gear in a corner and went to the side of the house.

I was behind them but went upstairs while they went into the utility room off the kitchen to use the sink next to the washer. I was heading to the bathroom, when from the corner of my eye, I saw something move in my bedroom. Gretchen was standing before the mirror, admiring herself in my Communion outfit. The only thing missing was the nosegay, which was in the refrigerator.

Hallowed Be Thy Name

The one good thing about receiving the sacrament of Confirmation was that you got to pick a middle name for yourself. For most people, it would be a third name, but for me, it was my second. I was the only one of the four kids in my family that wasn't given a middle name.

"You didn't need one," my mother said. "You were named after a saint. Your sister wasn't."

"Patsy Gallagher and Trisha McHenry don't have middle names because St. Patrick is their patron saint!" I protested.

"Goody for them," my mother said. She was washing, Patty was drying, and I was putting the dishes away, as we did every weekday night.

"Eeeiin," my sister pronounced the name like a pinch. She hated her name – Patricia Ann. I didn't blame her. But my mother's theory didn't hold up for my brothers.

"What about Freddy and Greg?"

"What about them?" my mother asked.

"They got middle names and they were named after saints!"

"They're boize," Patty was going to do everything nasally now.

26

"Boize are spethall."

My mother grabbed the towel out of her hand and shoved it into mine. "Go do your homework. Your sister will finish."

"I'm thorry." Patty took her 'Chatty Cathy' pose – arms bent at the elbow with her fingers splayed, framing her wide-eyed scary face – and shuffled out the kitchen, chattering, "Will you play with me? Let's play house. I wuv you."

"You're not funny. You think you are, but you're not!" my mother yelled over her shoulder as she attacked the broiler pan with an S.O.S. pad.

"I still don't know why they got a middle name, and I didn't," I grumbled, not sure if I wanted my mother to hear me. I had to at least get it out of my brain, or I wouldn't be able to fall asleep. She dropped the pan, letting it sink under the suds, took off her Playtex gloves, turned to me and said, "Sit down." I took a seat at the kitchen table, and she did likewise.

"Now, I wasn't sure if I was ever going to tell you this. And I thought if I did, I'd wait until you were old enough and ready to hear it."

"I'm eight!" I screeched. Ready for what? What was this all about?

"That's not so old. This is just between the two of us. Nobody else knows."

"What about Dad?"

"Of course he knows."

"So, that'll make three, me, Dad, and you."

"Okay, then. You have to promise that you will never tell anyone, especially your sister."

"I promise." Patty was right – I was adopted.

"Before you were born, I prayed to God every morning and every night that you would be born healthy. And he told me that you would be, healthy, and you know what else he told me?"

"No." Was I supposed to know the answer? I wasn't part of that conversation. My mother was making me nervous.

"He told me that you were going to be a boy."

"Huh?" This was bad news.

"So I was going to name you, Christopher Robert – Robert for your father –"

"WHAT? Even an unborn boy gets a middle name in this family! That's not fair!" I stormed out the kitchen as my mother called after me, "You've got a beautiful name!"

I ran up the stairs, into my room, threw myself on my bed and cried into the pillow. I could still hear my mother calling from the bottom of the stairs.

"The most beautiful name in the family!"

"She's right for once. You do. So grow up already." Patty was hanging over the edge of her bed reading her history book, blowing blue bubble gum bubbles and sucking them back into her mouth. She deliberately chewed, blew, popped, and sucked gum as obnoxiously as she could to irritate me.

"You grow up!" I screamed through my sobs.

"Tell your sister to come down here and finish the dishes!" my mother yelled, still at the bottom of the stairs. Even though we shared the bedroom, it seemed the only time our mother let us be in the room at the same time was when we were sleeping.

My name wasn't so beautiful – 'Catherine' – but everyone called me 'Cassie' thanks to Patty. She was three when I was born and 'Cassie' was what came out when she went for 'Cathy'.

Confirmation was in two weeks, and I still hadn't chosen a name. I'd been thinking about this since first grade when we learned about the sacraments. Every day for two years, I'd carry a name around in my head and take it for a test drive. I'd examine it for looks, sound, and compatibility with my other two names. After a week, if it was still on my mind, it was shortlisted.

After two years I had one very long short list. It was time to adjust the criterion. Since both my first and last name began with the letter 'C', all names beginning with that letter were out. When I explained this theory to my mother and sister one night during dishes, they did a very rare thing and spoke in unison and said, "That's just stupid."

By the time you got to third grade you'd already received three sacraments. Baptism, when you were barely born and couldn't possibly have any memory of it; Confession, which was embarrassingly horrific, but it made sense to me; and Communion was the pay-off for going through Confession, but it was torture of another kind that involved fasting and swallowing a dry disk of white flour. These two sacraments you had to make every week. According to my mother, it would become just another thing you had to do, like brushing your teeth. Confirmation was a one-time thing, and that made it seem all the more spooky. It required study, a ceremony, rehearsal, and somewhere a slap in the face took place.

Every morning for two weeks Sister Anne, the other third grade teacher, came into our classroom for instruction in the 'tenets' of the sacrament of Confirmation. Our teacher, Miss Connor, went into Sister Anne's class and did whatever Sister Anne told her to do. Miss Connor was new to the school and very positive and calm, which seemed to bother Sister Anne who was uptight and always in a hurry.

Sister Anne was short and skinny, yet she had a noticeable pointy bust line. Her face and hands were shiny and as white as the coif of her habit. The features on her face looked like they were traced on with black ink – black beady eyes, a triangular nose, and a lipless narrow mouth. I was so glad I wasn't in her class. Miss Connor was pleasant to look at. She wasn't a beauty, but she was the right size for an adult and wore colorful clothes. Plus, it was comforting to look at someone with hair.

When I first set eyes on a nun, it was from the back seat of a moving car when I was three. There was a group of them scurrying towards the church in their black and white habits. It looked like they were attached to each other. I didn't think they were real humans like me and all the people I'd seen up to that point in my life, who wore normal clothes. I thought they came with the church, like accessories. Sister Anne always brought that image to my mind. She ruined the name 'Anne' for me and Patty.

We were reading aloud together from the Baltimore Catechism: Receiving the sacrament of Confirmation meant that we were making our own choice to become a real Catholic." Linda Warner's hand shot up before we could start the next sentence. She didn't even wait for Sister Anne to nod or point at her, she just called out, "Sister, what does choice mean?"

"Well let me ask you a question, Linda," Sister Anne was at Linda's desk, leaning over her like a hawk, "Do you want to receive the sacrament of Confirmation? Or not receive the sacrament of Confirmation and rest in limbo for eternity and never see the face of God?"

"The first one."

"Which is?"

"Make my Confirmation."

"There, then Linda, you made your own choice."

Later that day, Linda told us that Sister Anne smelled like bad eggs and that's why she said 'yes' to making her Confirmation. Otherwise, she would have asked more questions.

There was a lot to memorize – the seven 'gifts' of the Holy Ghost, and the seven 'fruits' – those were okay. I could remember words like wisdom, knowledge, charity, and joy. But there was another side to the story. Our 'enemies' were the world, the devil, and the flesh. The 'weapons' we had to fight them with were prayer, sacrifice, and grace. It sounded like we were entering an uneven war.

Every ceremony at Our Lady of Perpetual Sorrow involved a solemn procession around the block with the grade involved, or sometimes the entire school took part. The student portion of the parade was followed by a posse of priests and altar boys in glittery silver and gold vestments, ringing chimes, and carrying a thurible or two of frankincense and a towering crucifix or cross, sometimes both. Behind this spectacle was the main attraction, a Bishop or Archbishop.

These events required a rehearsal, sometimes two, depending on how the first one went. Sister George, the eighth-grade boys' teacher and basketball coach, would stand in for whomever was the main attraction of the ceremony. Sister George was close to six feet tall and moved like a battleship on attack. She had an exotic look with olive skin, and violet-black eyes, and was one of the few St. Joseph's nuns who had eyebrows.

On rehearsal days, the school would hire a substitute teacher to cover her class. The few substitute teachers I ever saw at the school were middle-aged meek women. If they were assigned to Sister George's class, they were gone by lunchtime. This year Sister George covered her classes with police officers from the local precinct. My brother Greg, an eighth grader, said the cop in the morning read the Daily Times to them, and the one in the afternoon put his gun on the desk and just stared at them for the rest of the afternoon.

31

"I find that hard to believe," my mother said after the six of us had squeezed into our seats at the kitchen table.

"Why? That's what he did!" Greg shouted through a mouthful of chicken salad.

"Close your mouth, before you choke to death," my mother said.

"He did Mom!" Patty yelled, "I passed the class on my way to the girls' room and I saw him sitting there! Like a fat navy blue blob, staring at them with his feet on the desk." My sister puffed out her cheeks.

"As long as the gun didn't go off," my father said absently, quietly chewing, staring across the table at the light switch on the wall.

"Pow! Pow!" my little brother Freddy shot each of us with his trigger finger. "You're all dead!" We ignored him and lived.

"He's comin' back tomorrow," Greg said.

"Why? How do you know that?" I asked.

"Cause, he said, 'see ya tamarrah.'"

"I can't do another rehearsal!"

"You are soooo dramatic," Patty said.

"What's the matter with you, Cassie?" my dad asked while he scraped his plate with his fork, savoring every last drop of his meal.

"She slapped me really hard!"

"She takes her job sooo seriously," Patty said. Greg nodded.

"Why didn't you tell me she was going to do it so hard?"

Patty bit into a potato chip and with a full mouth said, "She's so beautiful!"

"So what! I hate her!"

"Pow pow!" Freddy fired at me again. I fired back at him, "Cut it out you little brat!"

"She's just getting' you warmed up," my dad said. "Is there anything else to eat, Betty?" My mother plopped a blue bucket of Herr's potato chips in front of him.

32

"Warmed up for what?" I asked.

"For the Cardinal," Patty said. "One year he knocked out a girl's front teeth."

"It was one tooth, and it was ready to come out and it wasn't the Cardinal, it was the Archbishop and enough of your stories," my mother said all this while she took everyone's plate away, except mine, which was still full.

"If you'd given me a middle name, I wouldn't be doing this. It's supposed to be our choice to do this, and I wouldn't care that I'd spend eternity in limbo never seeing God's face!"

"Finish your dinner while it's still cold," my mother said as she opened a fresh pack of Kools.

"What's for dessert?" Freddy asked.

"Did you pick a name yet?" Greg asked.

"No."

"Well, you better do it soon," Greg said.

"I will."

"When?" Patty asked.

"None of your business!" It wasn't easy to eat and defend oneself at the same time.

"What's for dessert?" Freddy whined.

Greg scooped a handful of chips from the bucket. "George told Tilman that she was going to assign names to the kids who didn't have one picked out by tomorrow," he shoved the pile into his mouth and chomped, still looking at me like he was waiting for a 'thank you' for the information.

"You could've told me that before!" I stomped out of the kitchen and up the stairs without waiting to hear what was for dessert.

After calming myself and making a really short list of names, I went downstairs. I'd make my choice that night based on every family member's vote. They weren't the most discerning judges, but they were all I had. They had to do.

"Catherine Theresa, Catherine Bernadette, Catherine Maria? Which one?"

"I like Bernadette," my father said from behind The Philadelphia Inquirer.

"Why?" I was taking notes as well as votes.

"I have to give you a reason?"

"It would help."

"Alright." He folded the newspaper, took off his reading glasses, and looked me right in the eye. I was ready with a sharpened pencil and spiral notepad. "I just do." He put his glasses back on then disappeared under the 'sports section'. I decided not to put my fist through it at that moment. He was expecting me to. I'd make him suffer. Catch him off guard.

"Marie. Not Maria," my mother was too quick with her answer.

"Why not Maria?" I asked.

"It's too Italian," she answered.

"But Marie isn't on my list."

"Make a new list."

My parents weren't taking this seriously. Understandably, they couldn't even remember their own confirmation names and they weren't that old.

"None of them." Patty was on her bed polishing her nails blood red and reading her history book. She always did more than one thing at a time. I was in my pajamas, ready for bed. Sleeping wasn't going to be easy if I didn't make my choice. My brothers had each picked a different name and Patty's vote was crucial.

"Why?"

34

"They all stink."

"You should talk – Patricia Ann Lucy! That sounds so stupid."

"I didn't pick the name because of how it sounded with my name. Nothing was going to sound good with that. I picked it because I liked the saint. Didn't that teacher tell you that?"

"Tell us what?"

"That you should pick a name because you like the saint, not the name."

"No."

"Then she should be fired. She's got a big ass anyway."

"That is so mean."

"So? Are you going to tell Mom?" Patty wouldn't stop looking at me. Now we were having a staring contest. I didn't have time for this. After ten seconds, I took the loss.

"I thought you picked 'Lucy' because you liked 'Lucy.'"

"The girl in the Peanuts cartoon?"

"No, the red head Lucy, the human Lucy."

"I can't stand that Lucy. I like the other Lucy, but I didn't pick the name because of a comic strip."

"Well, I didn't know there was a Saint Lucy. It doesn't sound like a saint's name."

"She was more than a saint. She was a martyr. You know what a martyr is, don't you?"

"Yea."

"You don't know, do you?"

"I do so! It's a saint that suffers."

"They all suffer. A martyr is a saint that gets tortured to death. Lucy didn't want to get married, she wanted to be a nun. But this important rich guy in the town kept coming around, trying to get her to marry him. He would say all these things like, 'you have lovely hair, beautiful eyes, gorgeous skin, beautiful eyes, bla bla bla.' So one day, she gets fed up! And guess what she did?"

"She punched him?"

"She yanked out her eyeballs and handed them to him. That's how much she didn't want to get married. So then the rich guy thinks, 'Holy crap! I'm glad I didn't marry that WITCH.' And you know what they did to witches don't you?"

"No. I don't." Patty was scaring me, and I was getting lightheaded from the nail polish fumes.

"They burned witches. But guess what? Lucy was inflammable! You know like when something is inflammable, like tires or rafts? She wouldn't burn! But they kept trying and trying, and she still wouldn't burn, and then they ran out of matches, so they stuck a knife through her throat, and then she died."

Patty finally put the cap on the nail polish, "Whew! That smells strong, right?" She started waving her hands and blowing on her fingers.

There was a knock on the door, immediately followed by the entrance of our mother.

"What do I smell?" She took one look at my sisters' fingers and snorted, "It's time for you to go downstairs."

Patty picked up her textbook with her palms while my mother wasted no time in opening the two windows in the room wider than they already were. Before Patty left the room she bent down and whispered in my ear, "I hope I didn't scare you!"

"What was your sister telling you?" my mother asked as she pulled the covers under my chin and tucked the sides under the mattress, wrapping me in tight, like a crepe. She sat on the edge of the bed, kissed me good night and said, "You pick whatever name you want, not what your sister wants you to pick."

"I know." I was too tired and confined to explain that she had it wrong. Patty wasn't telling me what name to pick. She was actually telling me a horrid story about a saint. As soon as my mother left the room, it came to me. The perfect name! I wouldn't tell anyone other than Miss Connor until it was official.

The next morning, we were given index cards and told to write our confirmation name on one side and our full name including, the confirmation name, on the other. Miss Connor said I had made a very 'individual' choice. When I wrote my full name on the card it looked like it could be the name of someone really important in the world one day.

That morning we would rehearse only the part of the ceremony that took place in the church. Our teachers were to stand next to Sister George who was sitting in the throne-like chair, where the bishop would be sitting, and hand her our card when we were kneeling in front of her. Just like the day before, Sister George was hitting hard. Kids were walking away with flaming red cheeks. Why was God allowing physical abuse under his own roof? If ever there was a time or need for divine intervention, this was it.

Miss Connor was looking out of place standing at the foot of the altar with the nuns in their black and white habits. She was wearing her short tweed skirt that she would wear once a week, matching it with different sweaters and blouses. Today she had on a blouse I'd not seen before. It was a silky pale pink with pearl buttons down the front and on the cuffs. As usual, she had on flesh-toned stockings and high heel pumps. Today, for the first time, her hair was done up in a French twist. The day before her hair was down, and she was wearing a red beret that she kept on all day.

When it came time for Miss Connor to stand by Sister George, the nun held her hand out to stop my teacher from stepping any closer, and with her other hand summoned Mother Gertrude, the principal, to the altar. There was a rush of whispers and gestures, both nuns digging through their long nylon pockets, each pulling out objects not visible from the middle of the church. After a few moments, Sister George, being the taller of the two, brutally attached a Kleenex to the front of Miss Connor's French twist with a large safety pin. Miss Connor delicately touched the tissue, smiled, and thanked the sisters, then took her place next to Sister George, her face flushed like all the kids who were, and were about to be, slapped by Sister George.

By the time I knelt before Sister George, Miss Connor's French twist was collapsing under the weight of the metal safety pin. When we locked eyes, she gave me a wink and a smile. I wasn't sure if she meant it for the sheer stupidity of the tissue or for my 'individual' name choice which was about to almost become official. Sister George was blessing and miming anointment with one hand and taking cards with the other, making eye contact with nobody on the earthly plane.

That all stopped when she read my card. She stood up, shoved the card in Miss Connor's face, nearly knocking her over, and summoned Mother Gertrude with her other hand. But when Sister Anne appeared in her place, Sister George shooed the nun away, sat back down, and glared at me as she went through the motions of blessing and anointing silently, with the slap at full force and volume.

Later that afternoon, during arithmetic, Patty appeared at the front door of the classroom. Miss Connor, who was still calm and positive, despite her ravaged French twist, greeted her warmly.

"Hello Patricia."

"Hello Miss Connor. Could I please speak to my sister?" Patty was at my desk before Miss Connor could answer. "Look out the window!"

That wasn't hard to do since I was in an aisle seat by the window. However, I liked my teacher and she'd had a rough morning, and I wasn't sure if looking out the window with my sister during arithmetic was an okay thing to do. The decision was made for me as Patty pulled me out of my desk, "There! See it?" There it was, our mother's Pepto-Bismol colored Volkswagen Beetle, parked partly on the sidewalk, directly below. "She's in Mother Gertrude's office! Somebody's in trouble!"

Before I could form a thought, I heard it – that familiar clack, clack, clack of my mother's footsteps in her high heel pumps, coming from the end of the corridor. Time seemed to stand still as the collective 'we' of the classroom listened to the approaching footsteps, accompanied by a rattle of the rosary beads. All eyes that had been turned to Patty and me at the window were now on the door, including Miss Connor's as my mother, dressed in a powder blue suit, a black clutch purse dangling from her wrist and holding a pair of black gloves, appeared next to Mother Gertrude.

We all stood as we were conditioned to whenever Mother Gertrude came to our classroom. She nodded and waved us down while she approached Miss Connor. My mother stayed at the door, looking like a catalogue model with her short black hair and red lips. A slight smile came to her face when she caught my eye. Mother Gertrude spoke quickly and quietly to Miss Connor, then walked over to my mother who was now frowning at something in the back of the room. Where was Patty?

Miss Connor wrote instructions on the board, then turned to us, "Boys and girls, finish the problems on pages thirty-four and thirty-five. I'll be back in a few minutes." When she joined Mother Gertrude and my mother at the door, my mother turned her frown to Miss Connor's mangled hairdo. Now there were two sets of high heels, my mother's the more commanding, to listen to as they faded… then disappeared.

Once quiet descended on the hall, the classroom exploded into vocal chaos, provoked by my sister who had been standing behind the cloak closet accordion door. It was May, the closet was empty, our mom was no fool and my sister was reckless.

"What did you do? You must have done something. Mom never takes off work!"

A circle had gathered around Patty and me. It was true. Our mother had found her calling with a job at Belle's Boutique. She'd started the previous year and she seemed to grow more beautiful and self-assured with each working day. Patty was playing the third-grade crowd.

"She probably had to close the store to come here. If she gets fired because of something you did Cassie…!" Patty was stopped by a new presence in the room, our brother Greg.

"What are you doing here?" he yelled at our sister.

"What are youuuuu doing here?" She snapped back, raising her awesomeness a meter with the eight-year-olds.

"Sister George told me to tell Cassie to go to Mother Gertrude's office. You better get back to your class."

"Did you see Mom?" Patty asked.

"Yea. So?"

"She never takes off work!"

"Well today she did. Come on, Cassie!" We followed Greg out of the room, down the hallway and two flights of stairs to the principal's office. Mrs. Klein, the afternoon secretary and morning Kindergarten teacher, was erasing something on the paper in her typewriter when we entered the outer office. Mother Gertrude's office was behind Mrs. Klein's desk. Her door was slightly open, just enough for me to see our mother attending to Miss Connor's hair.

Mrs. Klein was looking over her half reading glasses at the three of us.

"Mother was only expecting one of you. Just a minute and I'll find out which one of you she wants."

She pushed a button on a plastic box next to her phone and spoke into it, her voice reverberating in the room behind her.

"Mother, I have three of the Crawford children here. Which one do you want?"

She kept her finger on the button as she waited for a response.

Mother's reply, "Catherine," was heard from her office. The three of us were having a hard time keeping a straight face.

Mrs. Klein spoke back to the machine, "Okay then, Mother, I'll send her in." Mrs. Klein looked at Patty and said, "You can go in now."

Patty took a step towards the office when Greg pulled her back. "I was just playing!" Patty said to Mrs. Klein, who had returned to her typewriter.

It was the first time I'd ever been in Mother Gertrude's office. It was a dark foreboding room with a large walnut desk, which Mother sat behind. Four wooden high back chairs were set in front of the desk, occupied by Sister George, Miss Connor with a restored French Twist, and my mother. I was directed to sit, I'm not sure by whom, in the one empty chair between Miss Connor and my mother. My heart was beating so loud, I was sure the adults could hear it.

"Catherine," Mother Gertrude was speaking with a gentle firmness, "could you tell us why you chose the Confirmation name that you did?"

I didn't know where to put my eyes and stole a glance at my mother's profile, which didn't tell me much.

"Because I like the saint."

"What exactly is it about this saint that you like?" Sister George was leaning across Miss Connor and looking at me as if she'd just caught me urinating in public.

"He protects my dad and mom when they drive. They have statues of him on the dashboards."

Suddenly a lump was in my throat and tears were flowing down my cheeks. What did I do wrong? Mother was reaching across her desk, handing me a Kleenex. An earlier picture of Miss Connor's hair flashed into my head. I caught a sideways glance at my teacher who was looking at the tissue.

"Mother, is there any rule in the church that would forbid my daughter from choosing a male saint's name for her Confirmation?"

"To be honest Mrs. Crawford, I've never come across this kind of situation, but there's a first time for everything in this gosh darn world now, isn't there?" Mother Gertrude gave a victory cheer thrust with her stubby arm. Miss Connor and my mother giggled as Sister George objected.

"I beg your pardon Mother, but this is not a whimsical matter. We cannot give this girl permission to take a male saint's name –"

"Why not?" I protested, "you have the same name as my uncle!" I was looking her straight in the eye. We were at a stare off and neither was backing down. When it felt like we were both about to get on our feet, my mother put her hand on my leg and Mother Gertrude reached across her desk, with her short arm, an attempt at a stop gesture.

"Sister, Catherine has raised a very good point here," my mother said.

"She certainly has," Miss Connor joined in.

"You know very well Mother that I was appointed this name. I did not choose it."

"Well, that's not entirely true Sister, but now is not the time or place to open that can of worms." She was laughing nervously, trying to fill the uncomfortable silence, broken not too soon by Miss Connor.

"What's in a name? A rose by any other name would smell as sweet." It looked like she was going to say more and when she didn't, she sighed, "Ah me! I forget the rest. It comes and goes." My mother and Mother Gertrude broke into hysterical fits. My mother was stamping her foot and banging on the desk with her palm. With every other chuckle, each would start to go into a coughing fit and quickly escape it. You'd have thought they were watching The Three Stooges. Sister George was fingering her rosary beads, her lips moving quickly in silent prayer. Miss Connor and I were soon laughing at their laughing. Once the laughing died down and the women blotted their faces with tissues and blew their noses, my mother stood.

"Okay, ladies, I have to get back to the shop. Mother, I leave this decision to you and Pope Paul." She gave Mother Gertrude a hug and pat on the back.

"I think it's a good choice, Betty. I've always had a place in my heart for Saint Christopher. Catherine Christopher Crawford, it sounds like a name for someone who could do great things in the world."

Mother Gertrude was smiling at me so lovingly, I felt bad that I couldn't start rattling off the top of my head some great things I might do in the world. I started feeling even worse when she kept looking at me and not saying anything. Why wasn't my mother jumping into the conversation as she usually did? I soon got my answer when I saw her and Miss Connor over by the door where she was fingering Miss Connor's blouse.

"Maggie, where did you find this stunning chemise? You must have spent a fortune!"

"Au contraire! It was a steal!"

I should have known that she sold her the blouse! She had told me after meeting my teacher on the first day of school that she thought Miss Conner needed to dress more proper. Meanwhile, she was strutting around in her noisy pumps, big red lips and aggressive short hair, administering unsolicited fashion advice.

Sister George had not moved a muscle since she started her rosary. From a short distance, you'd think she was made of marble.

"Sister?" Mother Gertrude called to her, "Sister, Mrs. Crawford has to get back to work." Sister George slowly turned her head towards Mother and raised her left eyebrow. "Come, Sister, let's not let our differences get the best of us."

"Mother, I'll ..." my mother was doing her sign language for 'this situation is sooo troubling, only I can handle it. Trust me.' The three of us stepped back as she found her mark in front of the nun, who upon my mother's approach, pushed back into her chair and raised her nose. Betty Crawford spoke with calm authority as I'd heard her speak to doctors, pharmacists, grocers, my uncles, and even Father Tillman. She used this voice with only men.

"Sister, it's been brought to my attention that in your stand-in role as the Archbishop you have been unnecessarily 'forceful' in slapping the children's faces and as a mother of one these children, I want to know –why?"

"It's a standard protocol, Mrs. Crawford. The children need to be prepared for whatever punishment the Archbishop bestows upon them."

My mother looked over at the three of us on the other side of the room. Mother Gertrude was holding a fist under her nose and rocking back and forth on her feet, her focus on the floor.

"What more could the Archbishop do to them?" Miss Connor stepped back into the center of the room, "Is he going to break their jaw or give them black eyes, or concussions? He's a man of God. Men and women of God do not hurt children!" She grabbed a handful of tissues and turned her back to us. Her body was trembling. Damn! If Patty were here we could relive this moment for years to come. The mothers knew their roles; Mother Gertrude to Miss Connor, mine to me, and out the door – Sister George? Nobody cared.

Before my mother got into her pink Beetle she stooped down to my level, took my face in her silky gloved hands, kissed both my cheeks and said, "I'm proud of you. Now, I want you to remember that it's okay to speak up for yourself like you did today. But always remember to think before you do, because if you speak up too much people stop listening to you."

"Okay." This day was going on too long. I was drained. How could my middle-aged mother go back to work after all this?

"Tell me the real reason you chose Christopher."

"It was going to be my name anyway," I shrugged. "You said, if I were a boy."

My mother smiled and pulled me into a hug. After a moment the hug got a little tighter and she started rubbing my back with slow deep strokes, something she did when I was younger, when I was sad, sick, or just before her kiss goodnight. I could feel the knots in my chest unravel, releasing a rush of breath and allowing it to flow deep and slow from the soles of my feet to the ends of every strand of my hair, joining in rhythm with her breathing.

Suddenly there was a shift in my mother's footing, a sudden clench in her back, a stomach growl cut short. I didn't even have to look. I could feel that pull. My mother was looking up at Patty's classroom and Patty was looking out the window and down at her with me in the middle, between the two, caught in blows from both sides, as usual.

I pulled away from my mother, turned, and walked back into the building without looking at her. I was standing up for myself the second time that day, without saying a word.

Seeking Sainthood

Sister Irma Deloratta was built like a Mack truck, each leg the size of an average fourth grader. Sister Irma didn't speak; she roared. We called her King Kong.

She roared through morning prayers, the pledge to the flag, grammar, history, and geography lessons. She roared the loudest during arithmetic and even louder when you got the wrong answer, but more so if she couldn't understand your writing. When her roar couldn't get any louder or if it wasn't having the effect she wanted, she attacked.

The third Wednesday in September, 1967, the roars were echoing off the walls in room 209 at Our Lady of Perpetual Sorrow Grade School in Cloverdale, Pennsylvania, a budding suburb southwest of Philadelphia. Ten kids were at the two blackboards working on long division problems. These ten kids had the lowest grade on the previous day's math test and were now getting a chance to redo one of the problems they got wrong.

The remaining twenty-six of us were to correct any mistakes we had made on the test and then continue to the new mimeographed sheet of equations that she was handing out. The room was painfully quiet as we all focused on dividing as many number combinations as possible while King Kong stalked the room in her rubber soles, her rosary scrunched into submission in her massive palm.

It was impossible to tell what corner of the room she was in, or if she was even in the room. She had mastered soundless exits and entrances through the back door, which was always closed – as was the front. Initially, we could sneak a quick peek, but after most of us witnessed William McGrath get smacked in the head with the yardstick, nobody dared to move their eyes from their desktop. Not pissing off King Kong had become my life's work since day one of fourth grade.

After an indeterminate amount of time, King Kong roared for us to drop pencils and chalk – all eyes on her. We kids not at the board were told to point out the mistakes made by the kids at the board. Christine Livingston's hand immediately shot up. King Kong pointed to her with the yardstick, her signal that allowed and ordered you to stand and speak. Christine relished bringing attention to anyone's flaws, as she herself had none. She was extremely self-controlled, well mannered, and perfectly groomed. Her uniform and school accessories remained pristine and glossy throughout the school year. I knew this because she had been in all my classes since kindergarten.

"Gertrude forgot to carry her four, that's why she got the wrong answer."

Gertrude Pitelli and her siblings were track stars. They were all wiry and long limbed with tough olive-toned skin. Gertrude always looked like she put herself together while walking to school. Everything about her was crooked and messy, but dangerous and funny at the same time.

"I didn't forget. I just didn't feel like carrying it," Gertrude announced to the class. A muffled uproar ensued; some of us swallowed back our laughter while the brazen ones let it rip. King Kong pounced to the front of the room. Gertrude was ready for her, holding her hands out, palms down, enjoying the ripples of her transgression like a naughty late-night host. After a few whacks on the back of her hands, King Kong shoved a still gleeful Gertrude down the aisle while the rest us of did our best to put on sober faces, gnawing the inside of our mouths to keep from laughing.

The other nine kids at the blackboards were secretly correcting mistakes, careful not to drop erasers or chalk from their trembling hands. King Kong was no longer welcoming our observations. She was pacing the front of the room, her cheeks expanding beyond the confines of her white headdress. She was on the hunt and would soon find her prey – Steven Galbraith, a skinny, pasty-white boy with a head of thick jet-black hair that might have weighed more than his body.

"WHAT IS THAT?" She slapped her yardstick against Steven's messy cluster of numbers and lines.

"The answer?" Steven replied.

"THE ANSWER?"

"It's not?" Steven crumbled into himself. It was almost Christ-like the way he endured such pain and humiliation.

"WHAT IS THIS TWO DOING HERE?"

"That's what I came up with?" A nervous giggle escaped from his throat, sending King Kong into attack mode. "AAARRRGGGHHH. WRONG. IDIOTS." She marched down the blackboards slamming whatever skull fell in with the rhythmic pounding in her massive chassis. BOOM. BOOM. BOOM. The young craniums ricocheted off the black slate, expelling halos of chalk dust that crowned their small skulls before disintegrating and contributing to the malignant atmosphere of the classroom. Why no one's head had exploded into smithereens three weeks ago, we figured, was an act of God.

The rest of us sat shaking in our seats taking mental inventories for incomplete homework, un-dotted i(s) or scruffy shoes, and prayed for God to please open the ground beneath our desks and swallow us whole into its dark comfort. Only eight more years of this.

"I can't believe this monster is a bride of Christ," Shelly, my best friend, whispered to me from across the aisle.

"Yeah, what was God thinking when He married her?" I whispered back, careful not to turn my head or move my lips. Even though King Kong was engaged in knocking around the kids at the boards, being as still as possible was a survival instinct most of us were unconsciously developing.

"If He's everywhere, like they say, why doesn't He stop her before somebody gets a concussion?"

I'm not sure who whispered or maybe even wrote that, but it's what we were all thinking. It wasn't just Irma. Once you got past third grade, you were fair game for the angry and frustrated faculty and clergy. Fronts and backs of hands were smacked with rulers and wooden pointers for missing homework, talking out of turn, or maybe for just the look on your face. Boys were dragged around the classroom, church, and school yard by their earlobes, girls by their hair. Any mention of these actions to our parents was met with indifference: "She's only doing her job."

Or, they just didn't believe us: "Stop your nonsense! You know, lying is a sin."

There was no law or commandment against hurting children. All the hitting, shoving and pounding was for our own good. To help us become a good Catholic. And learn.

I did not want to go to school. I wanted to die and go to heaven and report to God and all his apostles what was happening in one of his houses and make him stop it before someone got really, really hurt. Steven and all the other scarred children in Catholic schools around the world deserved justice. And I would be the one to bring it.

But how? We'd been taught that God could take us at any time, but taking your own life was a mortal sin which led to burning in a river of fire for eternity. This sounded a bit far-fetched to me, but at the age of nine, I had no other information on the hereafter that I could compare it to.

After three weeks of careful deliberation, I came to the conclusion that I had to give God a little shove and make my death look like an accident. My sister Patty and I shared a periwinkle blue bedroom with flashy blue and green flowered bedspreads and matching curtains. Patty was in the seventh grade and in my view, popular and well-adjusted to school life. She was on the track team which practiced every day after school with Father Tillman, the girl's coach and pastor of the parish. This meant that I had the room to myself until dinner and could execute any plan without the threat of interruption or ridicule from my sister.

I'd come home from school, go immediately upstairs to my room, sit at my desk and do all my homework. When I was finished, I'd take off my jumper and climb out onto the window ledge in my full slip, white blouse, and navy-blue knee socks. I'd then carefully sidestep to the center of the ledge, release the fingers of my right hand from the window frame, and with my arms at my side, I would recite in my head a rosary while I waited for a big wind to blow me off or a brick to come loose so I could fall to my death.

After two days of window ledge standing, I decided that I didn't just want to die. I wanted to become a saint! Yes! I wanted to skip the pain and misery of grade school and the challenges and uncertainties in life and go right for death and onto sainthood. No more long division, tests, or punishments – just floating for eternity in a sea of cushy clouds with angels and all the other beautiful saints and God.

They would look just like they did in the holy cards – smooth-featured, pensive, donned in flowing pastel-colored robes with golden halos encircling their heads. We would be holy and good together as we peered through the clouds, down onto our earthly human friends. I'd have superpowers that I would temporarily transfer to the children so they could protect themselves from the jaws of the faculty and clergy of Our Lady of Perpetual Sorrow.

It felt like I already had superpowers standing high at twelve o'clock on my window ledge, feeling the warm beams of the late afternoon sun and looking across the yards and into the kitchen windows of the houses on our oval shaped block. At three o'clock Mrs. Cavanaugh would be prepping a chicken carcass, or the entire mid-section of some unfortunate mammal, for roasting. Directly across from her, at nine o'clock, was Mrs. Antonelli with a stove top of steaming pots, skillfully stirring and seasoning. And directly across from me at six o'clock, Mrs. Donleavy, a bottle of vodka by her side, mashing potatoes and arguing with the small black & white TV on the sideboard. There was something dreary, yet comforting, in the regimented manner these women performed their chores.

The last Wednesday in September, the routine was broken. I didn't see a pregnant Mrs. Warner, at two o'clock, drop the stack of plates she was holding when she spotted me out of the corner of her eye. Or hear her screams to Linda her middle daughter and my second best friend, to run to my house and alert my mother while she searched for our phone number. I was mesmerized by a cloud, shaped like a wheel, rolling towards our house. It was a sign. A sign from my patron saint, Catherine; She and God were coming for me!

My mother must have been in her routine, breaking open a head of ice berg lettuce when Linda banged on the door. I was silently calling out to the cloud, "Please! Hurry! Take me! Please, take me," when my mother burst onto the patio, Linda at her heels with a half-eaten gigantic peach dripping in her hand. Where did she find a peach, I wondered, in late September?

"GET IN THE HOUSE BEFORE YOU FALL AND BREAK YOUR NECK."

Two lettuce halves fell from my mother's hands onto the cement. I followed the rays of sun as they shined on their meaty white centers, and for a moment I pretended it was my skull cracked in half. The fingers on my right hand clenched the frame. God was giving me a challenge; I was sure of it. I was not going to let this holy and sacred feeling that had arisen inside me disappear.

My mother and Linda were staring up at me. My mother did not seem the least concerned that she would not be serving salad that night, nor did she look angry as I had expected. She looked young and beautiful, and for the first time, to my eyes – frightened. Linda took a bite of the peach, a trickle of juice drizzled onto my mother's bare ankle. My mother absently lifted her leg, pulled the dish towel from her apron sash and brushed her ankle clean without taking her eyes off me. What happened to that cloud? Suddenly I was overcome with dizziness or fear, I wasn't sure which, and dared not shift my eyes from the patio to the sky.

Was it my mother's beauty that was holding me to this world or my fascination with Linda's gigantic peach that didn't seem to be getting any smaller with each slushy bite? Damn! I could not let a soggy piece of fruit ruin my chances of becoming a saint! My mother was saying something about 'my whole life' and 'being foolish'. I think I heard the word 'love' but I was concentrating on lifting my eyeballs off the patio and into the yard where Darcy, the Donleavy's ancient chocolate cocker spaniel, was crawling under the white ranch-style fence that separated the back yards. After Darcy's bottom cleared the wood, she took a couple of victory steps then squatted and urinated in the middle of our lawn.

I did not want to make eye contact with the animal so I took my focus back to finding that wheel shaped cloud when from the corner of my left eye I saw Mrs. Antonelli daintily scooting across her grass, in all her lady likeness with full apron and bouffant hairdo. I wanted to shout to her that I hoped she had turned her burners off, but I thought that would confuse things and went back to my search, which was interrupted when I caught Mrs. Donleavy rolling over the fence, with the same lumbering grace as her dog. Would she also stop and urinate once she was over?

I didn't want to find out, so I tried to take my eyes back to the sky, but they were pulled to the left where Mrs. Antonelli was squeezing her curvy self through the middle opening of the fence. Had these ladies never climbed a fence? As if to answer my silent question with a "no," Fran Cavanaugh leapt into my vision and my yard with a high vault, landing on her two big feet.

What did they all think they were going to do? None of them had a ladder. They were wasting their time and possibly ruining their dinners. I needed to stay true to my mission. I carefully lifted my whole face up to the sky – an affirmation to God and St. Catherine that I was still waiting for them and to please ignore these ladies as I was.

"Stop your fooling around right now. This is not funny." Did I hear a little sob coming from my mom?

"You're killing your mother!"

My eyes flickered to the patio on their own, where Mrs. Cavanaugh was standing on the '6' square of the hopscotch my dad had painted on the patio for Patty and me. Her hands were on her hips forming two

Isosceles triangles with her long arms.

"Betty, do you want me to call Robert?"

"Don't Fran. He'll have a heart attack."

"It's a wonder you haven't had one yourself."

There they were going again with the heart attack. Somebody somewhere was always almost in danger of having a heart attack. And how was me standing on the window ledge killing my mother? Wasn't exaggeration a lie and therefore a sin? I couldn't think about the state of Fran Cavanaugh's soul, I had to stay focused on getting to heaven. Slowly, with utter reverence, I lifted my eyes, then my chin up to the sky and began a silent conversation with God but was immediately interrupted by screeches and giggles from the 9 o'clock end of the yard where, of course, my eyes had to go.

It looked like Mrs. Antonelli was stuck between the two slabs of wood in the middle of the fence and Mrs. Donleavy was trying to pull her free but kept falling on her bottom with each tug. At the same time Darcy was mucking up the works, trying to lick Mrs. Antonelli's apron. Mrs. Donleavy's yellow checkered dress was blotched with dirt and grass stains and Mrs. Antonelli's skirt was up around her waist, displaying some pretty colorful under things.

They didn't look like the somber mothers I witnessed just minutes ago in their kitchens. They looked like a pair of silly teenage girls with big breasts, having fun. Right below me on the patio were the slim and sensible grown-up mothers in modest slacks with understated breasts and serious, scrunched expressions and Linda, her peach finished, wiping her hands and face with my mother's dish towel. Where was the peach stone?

"Young lady!"

Fran Cavanaugh barged into my ears and head like a wrecking ball.

"You will stop torturing your mother and come down off that ledge this instant!"

Now I'm torturing my mother? I went back to my rosary, "Holy Mary Mother of God..." I would not let this horrid woman distract me and make me miss my ride to heaven.

"She does this every day." Linda was talking with a lisp. I looked down on the patio. My mother and Fran had switched their focus from me to Linda.

"Take the stone out of your mouth young lady, or you'll choke to death," Fran barked. Linda pulled the peach stone from her mouth. Choking, torturing, killing! Everything was dangerous and evil in Fran Cavanaugh's world. Her four kids were as mean and bossy as she was. Mr. Cavanaugh was our mailman. Instead of just putting the mail through the mail slot on the door he would knock and make someone come get the mail so he could hand it to them.

But I knew he only wanted to have a conversation with my mom. If he caught sight of me on my way upstairs or downstairs, he would always remark that I needed a good spanking. Thinking about this was really making me mad and wanting to jump on top of this monster lady. But that would probably count as suicide and or murder and I'd end up in hell.

"I see her," Linda said without a lisp, "she only does it for about five minutes."

Longer! What did Linda know? We were in the same grade, only she had the new 'lay teacher', Miss Parker, who looked like the Clairol Girl on TV. She had the same creamy vanilla skin, emerald eyes and hair like maple syrup that she wore severely parted on the left side and curled on the ends. Rumor was she was super strict, but she didn't hit. Linda's life was so much better than mine. I could start hating her if I wasn't planning to die really soon.

"Is this true?" my mother was almost screaming. She seemed to be getting younger. Was it because I was looking down on her or because, for the first time, she looked helpless?

"Answer your mother!" Fran snarled like a mangy German shepherd, the kind you'd see on Gun Smoke or guarding gas stations when they were closed.

"Why do you take your jumper off?" Linda was asking me. She had started playing hopscotch, using the peach stone as a marker. That was a good question. I think the urge to stand on the ledge came in the middle of getting undressed. I hated the jumper. It was heavy and plaid. Everything about it made me sad. Standing here in all white – except for my socks – I felt …angelic. I was beginning to sound stupid to myself.

Mrs. Donleavy and Mrs. Antonelli were now on all fours, working towards standing, laughing and falling over each other. Darcy had lost interest in the apron and was on the patio sniffing the lettuce halves. Oh no. What if Darcy went for the peach stone?

"What a pisser!" Mrs. Donleavy howled. The ladies were stumbling gleefully to the patio.

"I was ready to have you call the fire department!" Mrs. Antonelli squealed. She was taking off her apron, looking flushed and joyous.

"Aaaa! I'd have gotten Rudy's ax and chopped the damn thing down 'round ya!" Mrs. Donleavy shouted in her lilting Irish brogue. She looked like Little Orphan Annie with her mound of red curly hair and freckled face.

"And what if you missed? That'd be okay if you'd chop some of this off!" Mrs. Antonelli squeezed her butt cheeks.

"Only if I could tack it on to me own flat ass!" Mrs. Donleavy spanked herself, which set the two off into another fit of hysteria, quickly broken when they stepped onto the patio and into Fran Cavanaugh's glare.

"Well!" Mrs. Donleavy said, "fancy meetin' yoo here Francess."

"Humpf!" Fran Cavanaugh snorted, "I don't see anything funny about a child threatening suicide."

"Is that what this is?" Mrs. Donleavy gave me an exaggerated wink and smile.

"Sweetheart what are you doing up there?" Mrs. Antonelli was all heart and tomato sauce and gold hoop earrings. She looked like a gypsy. I was so happy they both finally managed to get past that fence.

"She's talking to God." Linda was skidding, not hopping, on my hopscotch. Her toes weren't making it off the ground. How did she know so much about me? She was getting on my nerves. I just wanted to watch these four adult women continue to act like catty teenagers. Linda kept interrupting.

Fran Cavanaugh gave another "Humpf!" then barked, "that's ridiculous!"

Darcy's aged ears lifted slightly and collapsed back.

"Honey," Mrs. Donleavy called to me in her sweet lilt, "ya don't have to go out on a window ledge to talk to God."

"You can talk to Him," Mrs. Antonelli chimed in, "anytime, anywhere, he's always listening. Isn't that right, Betty?" Mrs. Antonelli was adjusting her stockings, flashing us all her red and purple garter belt and panties.

My mom hadn't said a word in a long while. She was looking at Fran Cavanaugh as if she didn't recognize her. "Yes," she said without taking her eyes off Fran, "He is." My mom sounded unsure and strong at the same time.

"God doesn't talk to little girls that disobey their mothers. Isn't that right, Betty?"

Fran Cavanaugh folded her arms across her chest, for emphasis it seemed. She was giving Mrs. Antonelli the evil eye.

"Sure he does," said Mrs. Donleavy as she placed a Pall Mall between her lips and struck a match, "those are his best conversations." I figured Mrs. Donleavy would know about these things. After all, she talked to her TV.

"Dorothy –" Mrs. Cavanaugh addressed Mrs. Donleavy under her breath but loud enough for me to hear.

"They sure are!" cheered Mrs. Antonelli, interrupting Fran Cavanaugh, but not on purpose from what I could tell. She just seemed excited with the conversation and maybe really happy to be away from that hot stove.

"God loves a good argument," she was smiling up at me and emptying the dirt and stones out of her pumps at the same time.

This was the last straw for Fran Cavanaugh. Her face was rusty orange as she clenched her jaw and shouted at Mrs. Antonelli, "Angela puleeze!"

"Something wrong with your jaw, Frances?" asked Mrs. Donleavy, who was having a good time blowing smoke rings for Linda to catch. Where was the peach stone? I lowered my eyes to the hopscotch. Whew! Darcy was asleep on the '7' square, the peach stone on the '5'.

"There's no need for you or Angela to be here, Dorothy. Betty and I can handle this." Mrs. Cavanaugh pivoted to my mother, "Right, Betty?"

The cloud shaped like a wheel passed over the house as all the ladies, Linda, and me watched as my mother took in a deep breath, exhaled, turned to Mrs. Donleavy and said, "Dotty, do you have an extra cig –?"

"Sure as hell do!" Mrs. Donleavy parked her cigarette in the corner of her mouth, reached into her apron pocket, took out a red cellophane pack, shook out two cigarettes, and handed one to my mom and the other to Mrs. Antonelli. With her free hand, Mrs. Donleavy pulled a lighter from the opposite pocket and held a flare for the ladies.

58

All three took a full draw and exhaled at once, like a trio of chimneys. The yard went quiet as the ladies smoked. Mrs. Cavanaugh observed in horror and disgust from the other side of the patio and Linda sat next to Darcy, petting her. No one was looking at me. I was watching them. I was feeling the dark and cold coming on and wanted to go back inside, but retreating at that exact moment would reduce my entire scheme to an attention-grabbing tantrum when what I really wanted to do was to send a message. Yes! That's what I wanted to do. I was having a revelation!

That was something saints had, and now I was having one! I didn't want to die! I wanted to send a message! What was that message? Could I form that thought? I was going through my brain like it was a closet or a drawer, picking, tossing, picking, what was I trying to say? I lost my focus once again when I detected movement coming from the patio. Fran Cavanaugh was approaching my mother.

"Betty, I never knew you smoked."

My mother was a light smoker, but today she was looking like a pro. She brought the cigarette to her lips and sucked in deep. When she took her hand away from her mouth, a trail of smoke twirled before her face. She caught me watching her and didn't flinch.

"Well, I guess you never did know me, Fran," she said.

"Don't be silly, of course I know you." Fran reached an arm towards my mother.

"I never really knew you, Fran," my mother said, "until today."

Fran tried to get closer to my mother but stopped when she saw that my mother was trying to have a more important conversation with me.

"Why? Why? Why?" she said over and over until she finally finished with, "do you want to hurt yourself?"

"I don't!" I answered before I broke into tears. I knew I was safe because I was clenching the window frame with all my might. My mother stayed put, looking up at me, tears dripping down her face. I didn't know what to do. I was expecting Fran to bark the next order, but she seemed to be gone. I wasn't sure if Mrs. Donleavy or Mrs. Antonelli were still on the patio because my eyes were welled up and I couldn't move them around anymore.

I wanted to keep my attention on my mom, my beautiful, young, frightened mom who had just told off the neighborhood bully in a classy way. Her eyes suddenly were now looking behind me and she was nodding her head. At the same time, I felt a touch on my arm. Something was guiding me back into the room.

In a matter of seconds, I was standing in my bedroom before Patty who was gripping both my hands. She was in her track shorts and tee shirt, her face was glistening, and her short hair was going in every direction, but it looked good on her. Her grip was getting tighter, and I could see that her pupils had blackened out most of the brown of her eyes. We were both gasping for air and after a few moments our breaths were synchronized, and I couldn't tell if the pulse I felt beating was mine or hers. The more I tried to free myself from her, the harder she squeezed and the closer her face leaned into mine.

"What are you trying to prove?" Her breath was hot.

"None of your business!"

"You think jumping off a window ledge is going to change anything?"

"Let me go!"

Suddenly Patty did let go of my hands, only to free hers to slap me hard, across the face.

"Ow!"

"Listen to me. I die first. You understand? That's the way it's supposed to be because I'm your big sister."

"Okay!" I screamed before she hit me again.

"Do you promise?"

"I promise."

She grabbed me into a hug that was comfortable because it was better than being slapped or squeezed, but it was also uncomfortable. Her body was lean and boney and she didn't smell like herself. After a few moments she put her lips against my ear and whispered, "Don't you dare leave me."

The Safe Zone

My best friend throughout grade school was Shelly Evans. Her yard was diagonally across from ours and we were in the same class every year except for second and third grade. Shelly resembled my 'Ginger doll'. She was compact in the same way, her torso and limbs growing in pace as was her hair, which seemed to stay perfectly trimmed around her face falling slightly above her shoulders. She wasn't ginger toned like the doll, more like butterscotch with a tiny chocolate chip mole below her right nostril and a crescent moon dimple in her left cheek. We both had birthdays in September, and we were both really shy, which seemed like good reasons to be friends.

We would walk to school together, sometimes with my mom, or once in a while Mrs. Evans would drop us off in her car on her way to work at the A&P. After school Shelly would come to my house where we'd do our homework and eat saltine crackers.

On weekends when the weather was good, we would venture off the block into the neighboring streets of houses looking for new dogs, dropped coins or jewelry, hoping to get lost so we'd have the adventure of finding our way back home. Sometimes we just sat and read books or colored, in silence, which we did a lot in fourth grade.

Our teacher, Sister Irma Deloratta, aka King Kong, was a massive brute. A day wouldn't go by without at least two kids getting a beating. She never touched Shelly or me. It wasn't that she didn't smack girls; she did. Shelly and I were spared because whenever we were in the classroom, we held our breath and didn't let it go until we were out of the building.

In fifth grade most of the kids that had been in King Kong's class were put in Miss Bacon's class, including Steven Galbraith, a skinny kid who was a magnet for King Kong's wrath because he was really bad in math. However, he could have been bad in math because King Kong banged his head into the blackboard every day.

Miss Bacon looked and sounded like Ninety Nine, Maxwell Smart's partner, except her hairdo was more like Donna Reed's. She wore short dresses and skirts with flesh toned stockings that had a seam up the back, and a different color lipstick each day.

Miss Bacon loved her job. She told us so on the first day of school.

"I love my job. When I stop loving teaching, I'll stop teaching." She was sitting on the edge of her desk, legs crossed.

Linda Warner raised her hand.

"What would you do then, if you stopped teaching?"

"That's a good question. What's your name?"

"Linda Warner."

"You know Linda, I've never thought about it because I always wanted to be a teacher. But if I had to do something else, I might want to be an airline stewardess because I would love to travel and see the world. Wouldn't that be exciting?"

The first day of school with King Kong was a screech of demands. She held the yardstick in her hand the whole day, banging it on a desk or the blackboard like a threat.

"Okay!" Miss Bacon sprung off her desk, stepped around to the other side of it, and picked up her roll book in one movement that could have been part of a dance.

She even moved in a nice way!

"When I call your name, please stand and tell me your favorite thing about school and if you have a nickname, or another name you'd like me to call you."

King Kong referred to all of us as 'Miss' or 'Mister'. She never learned our names. We were a flock of sheep to be contained and controlled. According to King Kong, The Baltimore Catechism was our most important book and we had to memorize something from it every night. Miss Bacon told us to put it away, somewhere deep inside our desks.

"Sister Irma said we'd go to hell if we didn't learn everything in it," Steven Galbraith said in a shaky voice.

"If you really believe that Steven, then you can study it at home. But I don't think you should worry about going to hell. You're a young boy and you should enjoy your life." Steven's face looked too serious for a ten-year-old kid. He was nodding his head slightly as if the movement helped to process Miss Bacon's words. After a five to ten second silence, a rosy glow came over his face and his eyes were wide and sparkling.

"Thank you!" Steven said, "thank you very much, Mrs. Bacon!"

"I'm a Miss not a Mrs., Steven, and you are very,

very welcome. Now put that book away."

I wondered if Miss Bacon would stay this nice the whole school year. My sister Patty had her in fifth grade and was now in eighth grade, her last year at Our Lady of Perpetual Sorrow.

"She will, just as long as you don't do something stupid or rude. If you do, she smacks you on the backside, with her hand." Patty was at the mirror spreading wax on her upper lip.

"Is that Mom's wax?"

"She said I could use it."

"Huh." That meant that Patty went into her nightstand drawer and that was not acceptable.

"Take a picture it'll last longer." Patty ripped the wax off.

"Ow! Didn't that hurt?"

"So what if it did? Sometimes pain feels good. Like when Miss Bacon spanks you."

Now she was spreading the wax under her chin.

"Did she ever smack you on the backside?" I was getting a fluttery feeling in the down there part of my body thinking about this.

"Yea! Everybody got smacked at least once."

"Really?"

Patty widened her eyes, flared her nostrils and said in a deep spooky whisper, "If you get smacked it means she likes you!" She turned back to her mirror and viscously peeled the wax off her chin.

"Why are you doing that?"

"'Cause I'm mad at my face. Why else would I do it?"

I'd been hoping and praying for two years that my parents would buy one of the zillion houses they looked at on Sunday afternoons so I could have my own bedroom.

"Why the big puss? You should be happy you got Miss Bacon. She's a good teacher."

"I am happy!" I screamed as I stomped out of the room.

"Do you still wanna go to public school?" She shouted after me.

My sister's brain must have been put in backwards or on the wrong side of her head. She always did and said the opposite of what I wanted or expected.

I wasn't so sure about my public-school dream anymore. The public-school kids were looking kinda scary to me. Their school day ended earlier than ours. We'd be walking home in our uniforms lugging heavy cases of books while they'd be running around throwing balls or rocks and carrying sticks – even the girls. Some would start shouting, "Wahhhhh! Here come the 'Sorrow kids'!" They'd rub their eyes like they were crying. The older Catholic kids would ignore them or yell "Shut up," eager to get home, dump their gear, and change into normal clothes.

Once they had done that and re-emerged, from a distance, there was no telling the Catholic kids from the public-school kids. But if you got a little closer you could see the difference. It was as if we were breathing different air. The public-school kids seemed to be plugged in on low-vibrate, in a state of perpetual motion, slightly air-born and rarely silent. The Catholic kids were hesitant, solemn, quick to burst into tears, or anger – except for the kids in Miss Bacon's class.

"I don't want to go to public school anymore," I announced at dinner, the second week of school.

"That's too bad because I already signed you up," my mom said.

She had me for a second, but barely.

It was looking like fifth grade would be the best year yet. Miss Bacon stayed nice and interesting. The classroom always looked colorful and alive. Every month or holiday she would put up special decorations. On Halloween she dressed up as a witch. We didn't even recognize her at first, that's how good her costume and make-up were.

For Christmas we had a 'Secret Santa' and a party with punch and homemade cookies. On a few warm days in spring, she let us read our books for a half hour on the lawn in front of the Our Lady of Perpetual Sorrow shrine.

Patty lied about the spanking. But Miss Bacon might have been the first teacher that ever touched me. She'd give us hugs for doing good work or before a long break or weekend. Sometimes if she was helping you or talking confidentially, she'd put her arm around you. She told us she didn't have kids of her own but hoped to one day to have a boy and a girl. For right now, we were her kids. She never yelled or scolded. If there was talking while she was talking, she'd stop speaking until it was quiet. Problems seemed to take care of themselves.

For the first time, I didn't want the school year to end. I didn't want to say goodbye to Miss Bacon and go on to sixth grade, where all the teachers were nuns. My dream of going to public school returned, but I let it go while I enjoyed the first three weeks in June, which were always magical. Long days with no homework seeped into warm eternal twilights with a chorus of crickets, cicadas, and katydids enticing all kids – from all sides of the block and beyond – to run, laugh, and jump into dusk and sometimes darkness. We'd forget our differences and become one under the magic of summer's eve.

The evening of the last day of school in fifth grade was the summer solstice and the sun would not be going down for a very long time. There was a huge 'freeze tag' game going on and every kid living in a quarter mile radius under the age of thirteen and over the age of five was playing. There was something extraordinary about this night. I couldn't tell if it was coming from inside of me or outside.

I was happy with my face that day, my hair was looking good too, and I was running faster than I ever had, probably because my new sneakers fit my feet perfectly for once. The one thing I knew for sure was that I wasn't the same girl I was a year ago because of Miss Bacon. Miss Bacon, who treated kids like human beings and dismissed The Baltimore Catechism.

Charlie Cavanaugh and my sister Patty were 'it'. The safe zone was the white ranch style fence that separated some of the houses on the block. All you needed to be safe was a finger or toe on any spot of the wood. I was running through my yard with Charlie on my heels when I got to the fence just in time, set my foot on the bottom plank, turned, and shouted into his face, "Ha!"

But Charlie wasn't looking at me. He was staring at the girl sitting perched, like she was riding a horse, on the top slab of the fence at the other end. Her legs were wrapped tight around the wood and her upper body was rocking slightly while her lower part seemed to be pressing into the plank.

I felt a tingle in the 'down-there' part of my body. Charlie's milky blue eyes were bugging out of their sockets and a trickle of drool was dripping from his bulbous bottom lip. When he caught me looking at him, he sucked in the dribble, took a breath and screamed, "I'll give you both three!"

"Three what?" the girl asked. I'd never seen this girl before. Or maybe I had and didn't notice her. There was nothing noticeable about her.

"The count of three! You know what I mean. One. Two…"

I was about to run, expecting her to hop off the fence and follow me, but she stayed there, looking up at the sky. I followed her gaze and saw both the sun and the moon high above the clouds, parallel and a world apart. The moon was full, a frosty orb, the sun, a golden egg yolk. It looked like a stand-off, one waiting for the other to leave so it could have the whole sky to itself.

"The days are gonna start gettin' shorter now," she said.

Charlie was not interested in the wonders of nature. He slapped me hard on the shoulder then nearly pushed the girl off the fence before she kicked him.

"Kicking is out of bounds!" The boy's face was a wet beet. If he were twenty years older, he would probably have had a heart attack right then and there.

"So is pushing and slapping," I said.

"Didn't your mother teach you not to hit girls?" the girl asked.

"I didn't hit anybody!"

"You punched me!"

"I tagged you. Quit lying."

The girl stood up on the wooden slab, towering over Charlie and me, "You calling us liars?" she said before jumping, almost tackling Charlie.

He backed off, turned, and started running, shouting over his shoulder, "You're both frozen so you better stay still!"

"Is he retarded?" the girl asked.

"I don't think so," I said, with hesitation. She had a point. Charlie did not act like a normal kid. He was always angry, and his face was constantly leaking. If it wasn't saliva, it was tears or snot. "He's just mean."

"And disgusting, drooling like an old man."

We both started laughing. There was a gap between her two front teeth, otherwise she was the most ordinary girl I'd ever seen - short brown hair, brown eyes, straight nose, no freckles or other kind of marks on her skin, not even hair on her arms. She was just a little chubby

70

and didn't have much of a neck.

"I'm Cassie," I said.

"I'm Tracey," she said. "I go to Lynwood." Lynwood was the public school.

"You are so lucky!"

"Why?"

"Because you don't have to wear a uniform or go to church on Sunday."

"I guess," she shrugged. How could she not see her advantage?

"Or go to Confession. Confession is really horrible."

"Then why do you do it?"

"Because we have to."

"Why?"

"Because –" There were so many ways to finish the sentence it would've taken me hours to choose one, so I was relieved she cut me off.

"So, are we frozen? If we have to stay still…" She hopped back onto the fence into her original position and pressed her 'down-there' area into the wood. "It's more comfortable up here."

The tingling between my legs was now a vibration, a buzzing that needed a control switch to stop. As soon as I swung my leg over the top of the fence and my bottom touched the wood, the buzzing turned to an electric shock that wasn't painful, just extremely uncomfortable in a cheery way, but the moment was cut short when Shelly ran up and tagged us both free. The one time I wanted to be frozen! It was an unsettling feeling – yanking myself from the buzzing.

It stayed with me for a while like an echo and eventually faded as I ran around and away from my sister or Charlie, trying to stay safe. Every time I got to the fence that night, I was set free too soon. I yearned for that feeling, to go back in time and change the outcome of the moment I set eyes on Tracey.

First day of summer vacation was a downpour. I sat at my bedroom window looking longingly at the fence, worried that it would never dry, or worse, collapse under the weight of the pounding rain. If I let myself relive the moments with Tracey the buzzing would start again. When I was tempted to turn it higher and off with my hand, a haunting moment in first grade would flash in my head and the buzzing would rise to my heart and convert to pounding.

It was the middle of the first week of school and my mother was sitting on the edge of my bed, having just kissed my forehead and pulled my covers snug across my chest, wrapping me in tight, like a mummy. This was routine, and I was expecting her to say 'good night or 'sleep well' and get up and go, but she just sat there as if she were weighted to the bed. She spoke in a tone that was not quite a whisper, but far from full throated.

"It's a mortal sin to touch your body," she said as her chin and index finger pointed briefly to the center of the bed, the spot between my legs. "If you do, you must tell the priest when you make your first Confession."

Just like The Baltimore Catechism, she offered no opportunity for questions or clarification. She simply pulled herself off the bed and left the room – in darkness.

As I watched the rain slow to a drizzle and the sun peek out above the clouds, its rays shining on the tiny pools and drops of water along the top of the fence and shooting purple sparkles around the yard – my stomach filled with butterflies. The fence would soon be ready for me! On the heels of that thought, my heart skipped a beat. I was falling in love with an assortment of wooden planks – was that a sin or just sick?

Which was worse?

At church the next day I prayed for the salvation of my soul and that the fence would be fully dry by the time I got home. I had faith it would be because the sun was already at a scorch level at 9:00, the time I was woken too early for 10:00 Mass.

Even with The Baltimore Catechism out of our immediate vision, sin still weighed heavily on my mind. I couldn't miss Mass without the fear of hell haunting me.

Besides, there was no negotiation about it in our house.

Every Sunday the six of us would pile into the car for the one-minute drive to the church and the fifteen-minute hunt for a parking space. The church was always, no matter the season, stuffy, hot, and crowded. I had no idea what Father Tilman was mumbling about even during his sermon which was the only time he spoke in English. The 10:00 mass was the most popular because Father Tilman zipped through it and we were out by 10:40 at the latest. That was no consolation in my ten-year-old mind. How was it that public school people could sleep in on Sundays with no threat of a mortal sin on their soul?

Tracey was sitting on the fence when we pulled into the driveway. I had to stop her from doing what she was doing the other night before my family saw her. I pushed my brothers out of the way and made a dash to the end of the yard where I stood panting before a normal sitting Tracey.

"What's the matter?" she asked.

"I gotta get changed," I said.

"Okay," she said.

"Do you wanna come in and wait for me?"

Tracey hesitated. I couldn't leave her alone with my fence.

"Come on," I ordered. She jumped off and followed me into my house. "This is Tracey everybody," I announced for anyone who was interested. My dad was at the kitchen table sorting through the Sunday paper.

"Hi, Tracey," he said with a charming smile.

"Hi," Tracey said with confidence, as if it was an everyday occurrence for her, entering stranger's homes. She plopped herself down in the kitchen rocker, which our dog Bridget had laid claim to.

"You have a last name Tracey?" my dad was cupping a lit match to his Winston.

"Yea," Tracey was sitting back in the chair, rocking. Bridget was not going to like this. She was three-quarters German Shepherd and easily annoyed by children, especially girls.

"So, I'm going to have to take a guess?" My dad flicked his ash in the sink.

"I'm gonna get changed," I said to the two of them and ran upstairs.

When I came downstairs three minutes later in my hot-pink short-set, Tracey was sitting at the table eating a bowl of Cheerios. Bridget was back in her chair, pretending to sleep with one eye on Tracey and a low grumbling sound stirring in the back of her throat. My dad was hidden behind the sports page.

"Let's go," I said. Tracey put down her spoon and followed me out the door, with Bridget snapping at her heels.

"Where you going?" my dad called. I didn't know how to answer that question. I couldn't say to the fence, to the end of the yard. This whole operation had to be thought through. I was about to call a retreat and go back into the house when Tracey yelled:

"To the lake!"

"The lake? What are you going to do there?"

"Nothing!" I blurted.

"Don't fall in."

"We won't."

"Water's filthy."

"We're not gonna fall in!"

"Make sure you don't." My dad enjoyed irritating me and showing off for my friends. Whose idea was the cereal? Later he would tell me that Tracey's father was a heretic or something like that because he showed up at the end of a Good Friday Mass in shorts. He had been out running and stopped in to cool off, he told my father. He thought there might be a water fountain somewhere inside.

Shelly was sitting on the fence when we stepped onto my patio. Oh no, I thought, what if Patty was looking out our bedroom window? Or even my mom? Or both?

"We're going to the lake!" I screamed like a maniac as I ran towards her, causing her to jolt and tumble onto the lawn.

"You okay?" I asked.

"You didn't have to scream," Shelly said as she brushed the mud off her knees.

"Sorry." Why was I acting so crazy?

"We gotta hurry," Tracey called from the driveway.

"Why are we going to the lake?" Shelly asked as we ran across my lawn.

"Why do we have to hurry?" I shouted to Tracey. The lake wasn't going anywhere.

"It's a surprise!" Tracey said as she skipped ahead, her behind jiggling under her orange and white polka-dotted shorts.

The lake was about a half mile walk from our block, but Tracey knew a few short cuts through people's yards. There was a creek about six yards wide that you had to walk around or through to get to the main part of Clover Lake, where people would feed the ducks in the summer and ice skate in the winter. That day there was a fallen tree lying across the creek, extending from one side to the other. Tracey turned to us with a big smile, "Surprise!"

"What?" I asked.

"It's a short-cut," Tracey said, "to the other side."

"You're not gonna walk on top...?" I knew the answer before I finished the sentence. Tracey had already mounted the log and was hopping like a frog across the creek. Shelly and I looked at each other, then we looked at Tracey's polka-dotted chubby bottom dragging along the bark. When I looked back at Shelly, she wasn't next to me, she was at the edge of the water mounting the log. Who was I kidding? The buzzing had already started. I wanted this as much as they did, if not more. I practically jumped from the top of the bank onto the log, resisting the temptation to just rub in place. I withheld the pleasure and lifted my bottom off the log to meet my hands and soon caught up with Shelly and Tracey who were at a standstill in the center of the trunk.

"Why'd you stop?" I asked, although I knew damn well why.

Tracey turned her body around to face us. I was impressed with her agility, which was unexpected because she was pudgy and short-limbed. "Feels good, doesn't it?"

Neither of us responded. I was beginning to feel damp 'down-there'. My body was already delighting in the feel of the air and sun on my skin after being house bound for one day. Now it was on sensory overload. Tracey's nostrils were flaring. She took in a quick breath, and on just as quick an outtake said, "My mother checks my underpants every night when I put them in the laundry." Wow, that was a really personal thing to say to people you just met.

"Why?" Shelly asked.

"My mom says it's a mortal sin to touch down there!" I interrupted. I wasn't ready to hear the answer to Shelly's question.

"Is not!" Tracey said, "did your mom tell you that Shelly?"

"My mother works," Shelly said.

"So she didn't?" Tracey asked in an impatient voice. What difference did it make? I didn't want to stay in this conversation anymore. The buzzing was sending really good feelings through my body and I wanted to pay attention to them.

"You hafta touch, don't you? When you go to the bathroom and take a bath." Tracey said.

"Or you'd get an infection!" Shelly shouted in a high pitch.

"Yeah, it's okay to touch with toilet paper and a wash rag, but not with your bare hand, my mother told me," I said, hoping that would end the conversation.

"Your mother doesn't know everything," Tracey said.

"It's a sin when you touch to feel good," Shelly said. "That's what my dad told my brother." I was about to ask her which brother – she had three and they were really cute but mean to her – when suddenly the tingling sensation between my legs exploded into a circle of sparkles that got wider and wider and soared in every direction throughout my body. I couldn't stop it or make it slow down, it was moving on its own like lightening, rocketing through my blood cells so fast and hard it took my breath away. Then slowly, like a car with bad brakes, I jolted and jerked back to earth.

Whatever just happened felt too good not to be bad. If I fell into the lake and drowned today, I would definitely go to hell. Tracey was smiling at me. The gap between her teeth made the moment feel more exciting and dirty at the same time.

"You're not touching so it's not a sin." Did they teach mind reading at public schools?

"But it feels like a sin," I said.

"Why?" Tracey asked.

77

"Because it feels soooo good," Shelly said, "we're not supposed to ever feel really good if we want to get into heaven when we die." Did what happened to me just happen to Shelly?

"So what? You'll be dead," Tracey said.

"But in heaven you won't really be dead," I said.

"How do you know for sure?" Tracey asked.

"That's what you learn in Catholic school," Shelly said.

"Do you know anybody that's been to heaven?" Tracey asked.

Shelly and I laughed, "NO! We don't know any dead people!"

"I don't care what happens to me when I'm dead 'cause I'll be dead and it won't make any difference to me where I am." Tracey said, as she turned herself around. "I wanna feel good while I'm living!" She called over her shoulder as she slowly dragged her chubby self across the log. Shelly turned around to face me. She was much prettier to look at than Tracey.

"Maybe she's right," Shelly said.

"But she's only ten. How can she know more than King Kong or Father Tilman?"

"But how do they know anything if they've never been dead?"

Those were both good questions. The buzzing was starting again and my shorts felt wet at the crotch. Shelly's head was lowered and she was breathing heavily. Tracey was almost at the other side of the creek. A picture of Miss Bacon sitting on the edge of her desk, her legs crossed, flashed in my mind.

"I just remembered something Miss Bacon said!" I shouted. "She told Steven not to worry about hell."

Shelly lifted her head up; she had the biggest smile I ever saw on her face and her eyes were starry aqua pools.

"And then," I continued, "she said, you're young, you should enjoy your life! Who you gonna believe first, Miss Bacon or King Kong?"

That was an easy question.

"Miss Bacon!" we screamed at the same time as we rocked in place on the log, giggling, our chests and faces brushing against each other as we gave into the magical breathtaking feelings our bodies were giving us.

"You wanna live or die!" Tracey called to us.

"We wanna live!" Shelly and I yelled across the creek.

Tracey was standing on the other side underneath a canopy of trees, the color of emeralds, jade, and limes. The water and rocks between us were glistening so brightly in the sunshine I could see a kaleidoscope of fairies with every blink.

This moment, on this day, was heaven enough for me.

A Christmas Cringe

Sister Dorotheus spent every school day shuffling up and down the aisles of our tiny classroom in a Jack Benny pose – her right hand grazing her cheek, left arm folded across her slight chest supporting the right elbow – with a dazed, stunned look on her face while we copied our textbooks into our notebooks.

Today was the last day of school before Christmas vacation and the only acknowledgement of the holiday in our sixth-grade classroom was a black and white picture of the Nativity Scene our teacher had copied from the Spencer's Christmas Catalogue and hung above the cloak closet. The sole appearance of festive color in the room was the red thumbtack holding it up.

While the teachers and students in the main building were brimming in holiday cheer with Christmas carols ringing through the intercom into the halls and classrooms, we were sitting in silence, copying the "Twas the Night Before Christmas" poem from the blackboards into our notebooks. Our teacher had written the whole thing sometime between after school the previous day and 8:30 that morning. She was standing between the boards, beaming with pride as if she had Santa himself in her pocket.

When we were all settled, our coats hung in the cloak closet, book-bags emptied just like every other morning, except this one felt extra heavy and sad as we watched this strange teacher creature as she grinned and pointed with both arms like a magician's assistant and said, "For you. To copy."

This was her Christmas present to us. Fourteen, four-line stanzas. Each stanza had exactly the same amount of space on the board as the other. Every sentence was perfectly straight, yet there were no lines on the board and no trace of erasure smudges. Once she was satisfied that we were doing as instructed and had accepted her 'gift', she took her Jack Benny stance and set off on her daily cruise.

She was a youngish nun, somewhere in her twenties or thirties, but with her haunted expression and feeble gait she appeared both elderly and infantile. This was her first year at Our Lady of Perpetual Sorrow, the one Catholic parish in Cloverdale, Pennsylvania, and here she was, isolated in the old school building with twenty-eight sixth graders.

The building was an ancient fortress of granite and stone, separated from the main building far enough that in inclement weather a mad dash without proper accouterments was looked upon as self-destructive. Our classroom was on the third floor at the end of a long hallway lined with locked doors. This was the first year since the new building went up that a room was used in the old building, other than for the kindergarten classes that were held on the first floor. Entrance to the second floor was impossible so no one was quite sure what went on there.

Rumor had it that our classroom, which was half the size of the classrooms in the main building, used to be a janitor's closet back in the day before the new building was built. We were squeezed in tight, like a box of crayons, with four rows of seven desks, one on top of the other leaving little more than a two-foot aisle between the rows. The other clue was the one ominous window in the room that was eight feet from the floor, giving us a view of the bottom of the sky, heaven's basement.

Our one consistent contact with the rest of the school was once a day when an eighth grader delivered the morning announcements made over the intercom in the main building. Sister would either copy the message from the paper onto the board or give a nod to the boy or girl to read them aloud. The student would either look at us in pity or, if they were a mean-spirited sort, smirk at us like we didn't matter, cast out here like defectives.

The name 'Dorotheus' did not trip so easily off our sixth-grade tongues. It was foreign sounding without being exotic, and somewhat ugly. 'Dodo' slipped out in many of our efforts and became her nickname, which she was earning for other reasons. She was a pint-sized adult, not much taller than I was at the time, roughly five feet. Her complexion was a pale pink with a pebble-like texture that gave the impression that her skin was turned inside out. She had an ordinary straight nose and a small thin-lipped mouth.

Her eyes looked like they hadn't closed in a very long time. They were round lime green pop eyes. She had no eyelashes or eyebrows however, I had a theory that at one time she did, but they slipped down onto her upper lip and formed a slight moustache. She rarely spoke, maybe once or twice a day, and when she did it sounded like a cry – a Dodo Bird cry. For the most part she communicated with her excellent penmanship, through chalkboard notes such as:

"Stop Laughing!"

"I said, Stop Laughing!"

"This is my Final Warning!"

Handwriting was important to Dodo, and she excelled. She had

82

won contests throughout her scripted life. Certificates and medals of excellence were hung in discreet places – on the inside of the door of the supply cabinet and on the side walls in the cloak closet. It seemed this was her goal as a teacher; that we, one day, would be acknowledged for excellent penmanship; because that was all we did.

Around 10:15, William McGrath's father appeared in the doorway. Mr. McGrath was a taller and slightly thinner version of William and vice versa. Both had a head of tightly curled blonde hair, a white doughy body, baby blue beady eyes, tiny pug noses, and a heart shaped red mouth that looked permanently painted on. Undressed and wrapped haphazardly in a white sheet, they could have stepped out of a Bible photo shoot. Today he was wearing a navy jacket, white shirt with a red clip-on bow tie, and too much Old Spice. The jacket and shirt were a few sizes too small for him and it looked like he was being strangled by the collar and tie. However, he seemed comfortable, as if 'snug' was how dress clothes were supposed to fit.

Mr. McGrath had become a bi-weekly distraction. At the beginning of the year, he would bring William's forgotten lunch or homework. During a sultry spell of Indian summer in October, he brought a fan, which gave him another excuse to visit two weeks later when he retrieved it. On his last visit earlier in the month he brought a jar of jumbo dill pickles for the class. At first Dodo was uncomfortable with these drop-ins and would rush him out of the room with nods and grunts. Lately she seemed okay with his visits, on some foggy level, happy.

"Merry Christmas Sister!" Mr. McGrath bellowed. Everything he said sounded like a laugh or an announcement. Dodo's response to this man was to blush, bow, and turn slightly away.

"For you!" he guffawed as he thrust a gaily wrapped package before her, intercepting her bow, preventing her from turning away and causing her to do a bit of a double take as did we, remembering the start of our day and her only words since.

"Thank you," she cooed. The two stood staring at each other with their ghastly purple blushes.

"Aren't you going to open it, Sister?" Frankie Antonelli called out. Frankie was the tallest, cutest, and funniest boy in the class. I'd had a secret crush on him since second grade and spoke of it only in front of my dolls. Having him and my best friend Shelly in the class were the only good things about being in this cell block. The pinky pale was returning to Dodo's face, but now her eyes were twitching as she stared at Frankie as if he had more information to give her.

"Yes Sister, please open it." Mr. McGrath didn't like an Antonelli boy stealing his thunder and with a stiff extended arm, attempted a comforting touch on her frail back, the effect more a push, giving Mr. McGrath another opportunity to touch her as he guided her to a firmer footing. The two fumbled about stripping the package of its ribbon and paper, ultimately revealing a thick wooden paddle.

Mr. McGrath was beaming: "I made it myself!"

We spontaneously applauded. He somewhat bowed, his smile growing larger, enveloping his entire head. He returned his attention to Dodo, who was both mesmerized and weighted down by the unwieldy block of wood. Corporal punishment was acceptable at this school, but Dodo had yet to use it; there was no need. We were a pretty compliant group. Maybe it was the stale or lack of air in the building, dulling our senses.

"Have a look." Mr. McGrath turned the paddle for us to see an elaborately painted red inscription. We read aloud, as a class: "Merry Christmas to Sister Dorotheous."

Mr. McGrath flipped the paddle over.

"From Your Friend, William McGrath Senior." There was a scatter of applause that didn't take. Dodo and Bill Senior continued to stare at each other with frozen smiles. After a few moments they both turned to us, as if it was our move now to do or say something. Finally, William Junior broke the silence and shouted, "Thanks a lot Dad!"

"Your behind is going to be the first!" Bill Senior replied in a hee-haw chuckle that kept going and going, hoping somebody would join in.

"He's a sick bastard," Shelly muttered under her breath.

"He doesn't really mean that. Does he?" I asked to no one in particular. I'm not even sure I said that out loud or if someone else did or if it was a collective thought.

"You can try it out on me first if you want, Sister!" Frankie called out.

For a moment it looked as if Dodo was going to take him up on the offer. She had that look on her face that signaled to us she was at the cross path where the world in her head and our world met, and she had to make a decision. Mr. McGrath did that for her and whispered in her ear, then led her outside the room and shut the door. William Junior's entire head was a shiny scarlet Christmas ball, his curls now golden swirls of tinsel.

"Doesn't your old man work?" Frankie asked, as he did every time Bill Senior showed up in the classroom.

"He's off today," William answered, quietly as he curled into himself, trying to hide his head. Frankie was at the door, his hand on the knob.

"Shhhush! Everybody shut up!" He whisper shouted. Once the room was quiet, he slowly opened the door a slight crack. Sounds of smacking could be heard along with some muttering. We took a communal breath in and held it as we leaned forward. Frankie opened the door another inch and gently tried to peek through the crack.

Frankie was good at this. I looked over at Shelly and for a second, I thought I detected a sparkle of love in her eyes for Frankie, but decided to let it go. We all needed to have a good Christmas.

Some of the other boys were at the door with Frankie, trying to get a look. There was pushing and fumbling followed by a slamming of the door and a dash back to their desks. Dodo entered, flushed with the same smile on her face, cradling the paddle like a baby. She crossed to her desk and sat down on the edge of her chair, the paddle still in her arms, her face saying, 'I'm not here right now'. Our eyes were darting back and forth between Dodo and the open door where no Mr. McGrath appeared.

"You okay, Sister?" Frankie was at her desk. She didn't seem to hear or see him.

"Where's my dad?" William Junior whined, sounding like a toddler lost in a supermarket.

Frankie was standing with his hands on the board, slightly bent over. "Come on, Sister, give me some whacks like you did to old man McG!" Dodo was looking at Frankie, her face still dazed. "Come on, Sister!" Frankie's hands were smudging her perfect stanzas. His left hand on the 'the children were nestled...' the right on 'the moon on the breast...'. Once Dodo saw the beginnings of the violation of her work and Frankie saw her see that, he started rubbing his arms, chest, back and stomach all over the board, desecrating the entire first half of the poem.

Dodo got up on her feet, holding the paddle in both hands like a baseball bat. She was making her Dodo bird sounds and pointing with her chin and elbows at Frankie who was enjoying himself too much for comfort. I sensed a collective cringe, at least with the girls in the room. I looked at Shelly, who was looking at me and then we quickly looked back to the front of the room, where Dodo was about to swing the paddle onto Frankie's butt.

SMACK!

Dodo hit her target and fell back into her desk on the rebound. That had to hurt.

Frankie had a tiny butt. Dodo was leaning against her desk looking winded and fierce.

Frankie was still in his stance watching her over his shoulder.

"Is that all you got, Sister?"

"Why don't you sit down!" William shouted.

"Why don't you go home and tell your mother where –" Dodo cut Frankie off with another smack on his butt.

"That's more like it, Sister!" She swung again, with even more force. Frankie was still and silent as was the room. Dodo took a step back, looked at the paddle, then at us. For the first time since the beginning of the school year, her face was very much present. Frankie had not moved, but his body was shaking. Dodo turned and beheld the wreckage of her gift. She dropped the paddle on her desk then shuffled with a less feeble gait, out the door, and down the hallway to the Teacher's bathroom at the end of the hall.

The room was so quiet we could hear the bell ring from the main building. We were dismissed until the next year. No one moved. All eyes were on Frankie who stayed rooted and still, his body an 'X' shape with his palms on the blackboard.

"Hey Frankie, you okay?" one of the boys, not sure who, called to him. Frankie didn't flinch. Another boy started to approach him, but stopped short, turned back to us with a frightened look and gestured something to the effect that we should leave. We did so, quietly and with reverence, as if we were in the company of someone 'sacred'.

Walking to school on January 2nd, December 23rd was forefront on my mind. Maybe it was the scenery. Gray clouds against a gray sky. Sidewalks like a war zone, strewn with trees still green with strands of tinsel clinging to the branches, unwilling for the holiday to end. Just like me. I was feeling all gnarly and twisted and wished I was home, asleep in my bed. At least our tree was still up, giving the tinsel a more fulfilling life span. We were one of the last families on the block to take our decorations down. Every year my parents had the same conversation.

"Robert, when are you going to take the tree down?"

"As long as it's still drinking. That's the rule."

"It's not a relative."

"You go through all that trouble. Not to mention expense – for two weeks? That's just wasteful, Betty."

Shelly and I carefully made our way over patches of black ice crossing Beechnut onto Bishop with little baby steps, ready to catch each other when we started to slip. As we approached the school, we saw the usual group of nuns leaving the convent. We knew better than to directly turn our heads in their direction. We were skilled at side gazing, our objective to see if Dodo was among the clump of black nylon. When three or more nuns were traveling around the school grounds, they formed a triangle. The sister with the most prestige was the leader, the point of the triangle, and the other sisters filed behind in rows. The newest sisters made up the back row.

There she was – the last one on the left at the back of the line. We had come to recognize the nuns from a distance by their shape, size, and walk. Dodo did look more upright and quicker in her pace. Damn! I thought to myself. Not only did she not die, she's even healthier.

"She's still here," I said.

"She's not dead," Shelly replied.

Once we entered the classroom Dodo was at the board (her favorite place), writing (her favorite activity), the date in her perfect penmanship. William McGrath was fumbling with his galoshes that refused to leave his feet, a trickle of drool in the cleft of his chin. I had tried to imagine that afternoon for William, when he came home from school. Did he tell his mother about the paddle? Maybe she already knew. Maybe Mr. McGrath had given her a paddle for Christmas. Maybe he had a whole paddle woodshop in the basement.

Frankie was taking off the same coat he'd been wearing the last day of school. I was looking for a hint of wisdom or martyrdom in his face or stature. After that brutal Christmas Eve's eve, how could he not be changed? I was, and I was just an observer. I had witnessed violence and internalized it. Frankie caught me in a stare and winked. Nothing had changed. He was the same cute, funny Frankie.

I sat at my desk, smack dab in the middle of the classroom, next to Shelly. Dodo's back was still to the room, we were all now at our desks waiting for her to step away from the board so we could see the complete instructions. Once Dodo turned around the entire room took a short sharp breath and held it in paralysis. This sister was not Dodo.

This nun's skin was olive toned, and she had dark eyebrows and full sets of eye lashes framing large brown almond-shaped eyes that were securely set in her head, not bulging out and refusing to close, like Dodo's. Under the date she had written, 'Sister Jeanne d' Arc' and was now pointing at it. She then pointed at the other information she so carefully had written.

"Arithmetic: Pages 38 – 45, read, do problems in book, and copy all problems and text into copybook." A collective groan erupted from the room. I folded my arms on my desk and dropped my head into them. Nooooo! I screamed inside my brain and soul. A cry was traveling from my lungs towards my throat but was brought to a stop by a tinny dinging sound outside my skull. I pulled my head out of my arms and sat up to see the new teacher, who was sitting at her desk banging with her palm on what looked like the kind of bell some small stores and dry cleaners had on their counter for customers to ring when they needed service, and the clerks were in the back on an extended break eating and smoking.

"What happened to Sister Dorotheus?" Frankie called out. He was in the first seat next to her desk, so he wasn't really calling out, it was more a conversational volume. The nun looked at him with downcast eyes, flared her nostrils, then turned her head with an upswing back to the room. I took a closer look at her face, focusing on her nose now that her nostrils were back in place. It was a flat upside-down triangle, flaring at the bottom. It was the smallest of all her facial features, maybe too small for her face, which was the widest at the cheek-bones.

"Your handwriting's just like hers, Sister," Frankie wasn't giving up. He turned to the room, "Right? Just like Dodo's! Exactly." I hadn't noticed at first, but he was right.

It was down-right spooky.

"Was the ghost of Dodo's handwriting inside the board?" I asked Shelly, but loud enough for anyone in the middle clump of the room to hear. I thought it was a funny and interesting thing to say.

"Yeah! It's making her write like her!" Shelly added.

Soon the dinging started again, but some of us decided to ignore it. We weren't store clerks neglecting our duties, drinking and smoking in the back room. How dare she? We were kids on the day after Christmas vacation, and our blood streams were teeming with glazed ham and chocolate kisses, and our minds were on the toys left behind in our bedrooms, waiting for us to come home and play with them. We weren't ready to sit still in silence copying words and numbers that meant nothing to us. We needed stimulation!

There was a knock at the door. The room went quiet. All eyes were on the door, including the new teacher's. This knock was not recognizable to us. The announcement person would knock and open at the same time, eager to get their dealings with Dodo over with and out of the building. Most of the time, the door was left open. Dodo had little awareness of her surroundings. There was another slower, louder, knock. Now our new teacher was on her feet, at her desk casting a stronger, more serious stare at the door as if it could make the knocking stop. When the knocking turned to kicking, the nun stepped away from her desk, took a step towards the door as Frankie jumped out of his desk, leaped to the door and pulled it open. There stood skinny Gertrude Pitelli balancing a messy stack of books and papers in her arms and holding the whole pile in place with her long, belligerent chin. A note was sticking out of one hand which Frankie snatched and handed to Sister Jeanne.

After reading the note, with Frankie over her shoulder reading along, Sister pointed to Gertrude, then pointed to the one empty desk at the back of the room. She then sat down and started a rosary. The note was most likely from the principal's office telling Sister Jeanne that this student was being transferred from another sixth-grade class to hers. Gertrude didn't move.

"What?" She shouted over her tower of books to Jeanne d' Arc, whose lips were moving in silent prayer. Frankie was back in his desk, laughing.

"What's so funny?" Gertrude asked, daring him.

"None of your beeswax," he answered.

"Yeah it is," Gertrude dropped her arms, the pile of weathered textbooks and notebooks collapsing to the floor as she puffed out her chest, clenched her fists, and took a threatening step towards Frankie.

"Stop! Stop! Stop!" Jeanne d' Arc was on her feet dinging the bell.

A black cloud of dread collapsed on top of me. Oh no. With her silence I was telling myself that perhaps this sister was shy and gathering her thoughts to speak to us in a full voice, with a logical sequence of words, sometime soon, perhaps after lunch. That hope was now shattered. Here was another monosyllabic teacher! Another young, mentally indisposed woman who did not think this career move all the way through.

She pointed to Frankie and then to the desk in the back, "You go." She then pointed to Gertrude and to Frankie's desk, "You go." I wasn't totally sure these were her exact words, but it was clear that she wanted Frankie in the back of the room away from her and Gertrude in the front, a move Frankie was not happy with.

"Nah Sister, you can't put me in the back! I got bad eyes. I gotta be close to the board!"

"Move, grease ball!" Gertrude was pushing her books and papers with her feet towards Frankie's desk. Frankie kicked at the mound, sending it scattering away from his desk. Gertrude started kicking Frankie's legs and desk.

Before it got really ugly, Sister was banging at the bell again and screeching, "Stop! Stop! Stop!"

"Alright! I'm going. You're gonna be sorry, Sister."

"Why should she be sorry?" The two were on their feet, Gertrude's chin meeting Frankie's chest.

"'Cause you stink." He stepped away from her and back to his desk and started gathering his things.

There was nothing Gertrude could do until Frankie was out of her way. She just stood there watching him, looking at us looking at her, then back to Frankie and over to Jeanne d'Arc, who was clenching her rosary with one eye on the Frankie/Gertrude debacle, one on us, and her third eye on the clock on the back wall.

I didn't know Gertrude. She'd been in my class in first and fourth grade, but I don't remember ever having a conversation with her. I appreciated her from a distance because there was an element of danger and comedy about her. However, I didn't know how to relate to someone responsible for such stimulating relief up close and personal.

The Pitelli kids were champion runners, the only sport that brought money into the parish. August through November they were Our Lady of Perpetual Sorrow royalty. The rest of the year they were considered juvenile delinquents. Gertrude had a condition where she wasn't afraid of anything. She'd sneak into the church through the rectory, drink the altar wine and eat the hosts if she didn't have a lunch. The whole family looked like praying mantises – flat, long, olive skinned with skinny, pointy noses and oval eyes that reflected the hue of their skin to the minute. Gertrude's mop of straw-colored hair looked like she cut it while watching T.V.

Once Gertrude and Frankie were settled in their desks, I looked at the clock – 9:15. Did time just stop? The new Dodo was still sitting at the desk, staring straight ahead, her lips quivering in prayer, her fingers rubbing the beads like they were little magic lamps with the power to transport her away to anywhere but where she was.

It was a dreary three hours and they passed, slowly. The new Dodo had written, like her predecessor, all instructions on the blackboard. The morning ticked along slowly without too many disruptions. We copied new spelling words and used them in sentences that we made up. We read a chapter in our history book on the Civil War and answered the questions at the end, then wrote the new vocabulary words, places, and things in our notebook. We worked independently, alone, on our own, isolated in a crowded room.

Mother Gertrude Helene greeted us from the front of the classroom when we filed in after lunch. She was a kind, strong, square-jawed figure. She reminded me of a chubby Gumby or my Uncle Bob, one of my father's four brothers. Gertrude ran up to her and gave her a hug as soon as she walked in the room. There was a bond there because of the shared name and Gertrude had played it to the max since first grade.

"There's my girl!" The two were almost head to head and Gertrude was whispering in her ear. Mother was listening with a confused furrowed brow, a kind smile, a slight stoop to the side. Where was Jeanne d' Arc? Had she quit already? Mother patted the girl's back and stood straight, eager to get back to the new building and on with her day. "Good afternoon boys and girls."

We replied in unison, "Good afternoon, Mother Gertrude Helene."

"Did you have a nice Christmas?" There was a mumbling of "yeses, okays," and "sortas." We knew it was a rhetorical question.

"It's so nice to see everybody, and it looks like everyone is here today. No absences. Isn't that terrific? I understand the announcements didn't make it over here this morning, so I'm bringing them to you in person. How's that for service?" She chuckled and we joined her for a couple more chuckles as she looked to the doorway.

She continued, "The announcement this morning was a welcome back to all the students and faculty of Our Lady of Perpetual Sorrow. Furthermore, I hope you gave thanks to the Lord for all you received this holiday?" Mother's eyes widened as she nodded her head, a silent beckon to join her in the nodding. Christine Livingston, who was in the first seat in the row on the other side of the teacher's desk, raised her hand.

"Yes, Christine? Oooo! I see some sparkles on your arm. Did you get a new charm for your bracelet?"

"Yes I did, Mother! It's a horse. I start horseback riding lessons this week." Mother was holding Christine's hand, examining the bracelet, "Isn't that lovely!"

94

Campion

"I got a watch too, but my mother said I could only wear one at a time to school – the watch or the charm bracelet. In case I lose it or somebody tries to steal it."

Mother dropped Christine's hand and took a step back, "Are you suggesting there are criminals at this school, Christine?"

"Not criminals, just kids that steal."

"Well, I hope you're wrong about that." Mother looked sad and a little shorter as she looked at the tiny crowded class of sixth graders and meekly asked, "Would anyone else like to tell us about their Christmas?"

Christine's hand was the only one that went up. Mother saw it but looked pleadingly at the rest of us before saying, "Yes, Christine?"

"I didn't get to finish before. I also got a pink and blue pastel kilt with a matching blue beret to go with it; a sparkle paint set; wide-eyed moppet pictures for my room – " As she was listing her litany of riches, Mother was at the door looking over and down the hallway. Where was Jeanne d' Arc?

"Thank you, Christina, Santa was certainly generous to you. I'm sure you gave thanks –"

"I lit five candles at church –"

"Very good, we've heard enough from you, Christina, so please sit down and let someone else have a turn." Christine wasn't standing.

"I am sitting, Mother."

"Who else would like to tell us about their Christmas? Francis Antonelli? Where is he - he used to be in the front –"

"I'm back here, Mother!"

"There you are! Francis, tell us one thing – we'll keep it short so others – tell us about your dinner. For those of you that may not know this, Mrs. Antonelli is a wonderful cook. Tell us about Christmas dinner." Mother made herself slightly comfortable half sitting, half

95

leaning on the edge of the teacher's desk.

"We had ham and a bunch of other stuff, and my Uncle Nick was there and so was my Aunt Violet and Uncle David and their four brats."

That got a laugh. Mother just raised her eyebrows and height.

"I meant kids, Mother."

I eyed Sister Jeanne coming into the corridor from the back stairway. She was walking slowly, with dread it seemed. When she noticed that our attention was on the front of the room and kids were raising their hands her steps became even more tentative.

When she finally arrived in the doorway and saw Mother Gertrude, two rosy pink circles flashed onto her cheekbones.

"Well then! Here is our Sister Jeanne d' Arc! Sister, we were just talking about Christmas. Children, Sister Jeanne has taught in schools in the city of Philadelphia. Isn't that right, Sister? Tell your students about those schools. I'm sure they'd be interested to hear all about a city school." Mother took a step back, giving Jeanne d' Arc the floor. Jeanne d' Arc looked at us and then to Mother and then back to us.

"What would you like to know?" She asked us in a soft but full voice. Gertrude was the first and only person to raise her hand. Jeanne d' Arc nodded at her.

"What schools did you teach at?"

"I taught at Saint Michaels and Our Lady of Angels."

"Why did you stop teaching at them?" Gertrude asked.

"Because I was assigned to your school. When you're a sister, a nun, the Archdiocese places you in the school that it thinks bests suits you and the school. I didn't decide to stop teaching at the schools. The Archdiocese decided for me."

There was silence. Mother was brushing her sleeves. Jeanne d' Arc's eyes were twitching. I couldn't stand it! I raised my hand, not sure what would come out of my mouth. Jeanne d' Arc nodded at me.

"What grade did you teach, Sister?" Now I had pink blotches on my cheeks.

"Good question!" Shelly whispered to me.

"I taught second grade."

"That was a very good question!" Mother was smiling at me with a stiff open mouth. She was trying to remember my name.

I wanted to know if Sister Jeanne taught second grade in both schools, but was hoping someone else would ask, and if they didn't, then I would. Mother was looking over me, "There's a hand up back there, Sister. Mr. Antonelli, Mrs. Antonelli is a wonderful cook, Sister."

"Did you teach second grade in both schools, Sister?" Frankie and I were on the same wavelength that day.

"I did. Yes."

"Then we must look big and scary to you!" Frankie shouted. The whole class, including Mother, broke out in laughter. Jeanne d' Arc was smiling. Mother took this as a good time to go, leaving on a high note, as Saint Joseph nuns were trained to do.

"Well, I'll let you get better acquainted and on with your day –"

"Mother, don't go! I have a question for you!" Mother stopped at the door. "What is it, Francis?"

"What happened to Sister Dorotheus?" All the height and spirit Mother had regained in those last few minutes seemed to have drained from her; she looked almost shriveled.

Gertrude turned fully around in her seat, faced the back of the room and snarled, "None of your beezwax!"

"Now now, Gertrude, let's be polite," Mother said, sounding out of breath.

"But it is none of his business. Right, Mother?" Gertrude asked.

"Well, that depends. Why are you asking, Francis?"

"I just wanna know I guess." Did he think it had something to do with him?

"Who else would like to know?" We all raised our hands with such a force it almost knocked her over. My heart was thumping in my chest – lub dub, lub dub. I hadn't thought much about Dodo since early morning. During lunch, Shelly and I talked about Gertrude and Jeanne d' Arc. We were trying to come up with a nickname for her. I'd forgotten about what we said in the morning – "She didn't die. She's not dead." And how I prayed for her not to come back! Did I pray for her to die? I was trying to remember. I looked over at Shelly. Her eyes were teary. Why was Mother taking so long to answer?

Finally, Mother stepped back into the room. "Very well," she said, pulling herself back to her full height, "Sister Dorotheus had to take a leave of absence because she had some personal issues to take care of. So, Sister Jeanne will be your teacher – for now."

All eyes were on Jeanne d' Arc. Would she talk normally once Mother left the classroom or would she revert to silence and bell banging? Was Sister Dorotheus really alive? Would we ever see her again? If not, was it my fault? So much had happened in one day and it was only 1:15.

"Are there any more questions?" Mother asked from the doorway. We all looked to each other, hoping someone had a question that had an answer that could be put into words.

The Red Queen in Black and White

Our new teacher was standing in the doorway at the back of the classroom looking up at the door frame. Her arms were folded and tucked into her black nylon sleeves; her chin lifted high and proud. She could have been posing for a holy card or a film promo. Her profile with its aquiline nose, high cheekbones, pearly white complexion and lips like two juicy sections of a pink grapefruit was stunning! Why, I wondered, would such a beautiful woman enter a convent? She did not look like a real nun. She looked more like a movie star playing the role of a nun.

After another long fifteen seconds, an arm slowly emerged from the nylon tunnel, and, led by a pearly white index finger, extended to the top of the door frame, touched down on the wood, made a swift swipe from corner to corner, then circled back down to meet her eyes. A look of disgust, evident from where I stood in the front of the room, crossed over her face, a nostril flare and downward turn of the mouth, a split-second frown, as she reached into her pocket with her other hand and pulled out a white handkerchief. Making her way to the front of the room, she wiped her finger clean, folded the hanky into a neat square, and dropped it into the waste-basket by her desk.

"Whaaaaa?" all our faces and upper bodies implied. Why would anyone throw away a perfectly good handkerchief instead of washing it? Why fold it before throwing it away? Didn't you have to take a vow of poverty to become a nun?

At that moment the principal, Mother Gertrude Helene, a stout square-shaped woman who swept through the halls and grounds of the school like a tumble-weed, walked through the front door.

"Good morning, Sister." She gave a cursory nod in our direction, "Young ladies."

"Good morning, Mother Gertrude... Helene." We were never quite sure if we should include the Helene, as Mother was always in a hurry to get to her next moment. Sounding out her full name took seconds off her schedule.

"I see, Sister, you and your girls have met."

"Not officially, Mother. I was waiting –" Her voice was just as I expected, lower pitched with accentuated diction.

"Very well, then," Mother cut her off. "Girls, may I introduce Sister Ursula, our new teacher for you seventh-grade girls. Sister Ursula came to us over the summer, and we are very happy to welcome her to her new home. I am sure you will be on your best behavior and show her what lovely young ladies we have here at Our Lady of Perpetual Sorrow." A perplexed look appeared on her face as she glanced again at the thirty-eight of us who were standing along the walls of the classroom, weighted with text books and leather shoulder bags.

Linda Warner raised her hand. Linda always had a question. It was her philosophy in life to ask questions whenever an opportunity presented itself, and if it didn't, she created one. Every faculty member and clergy knew Linda by name, having been queried by her several times in her seven and a half years at the school.

"Yes, Linda?" Mother looked at her pocket watch, then up at the clock.

"What happened to Sister Agnes?"

This was one of those times that Linda's question reflected the collective mind of the class. The seventh-grade girls' teacher for the past ten years was the beloved Sister Agnes Mary, whom I was looking forward to having as a teacher. My older sister Patty and her friends assured me that any damage done in sixth grade, with having two unqualified, fragile young nuns as teachers, would be wiped out within one year under Sister Agnes's watch. She would make every subject a fun and meaningful challenge, and, once conquered, your self-confidence and self-esteem grow beyond your expectations. Plus, you could talk and complain about the most personal issues and she would listen and not judge or lecture you. And, what was said to Sister Agnes, stayed with Sister Agnes.

"I wish she was my mother," Patty had said a few times that year and continued to say over the next five years whenever our mother and she bumped heads or hearts.

"Sister Agnes was transferred to another parish by the Archdiocese." Mother's gaze was now facing downward, into the wastebasket, as she continued, "We shall miss her." She bent down, reached into the bin, pulled out the discarded handkerchief, gave it a brush and put it in her pocket. A silent sigh of relief for the rescued hanky traversed the perimeter of the room.

Mother returned her focus to us. "But we will keep her in our thoughts and pray that she finds as much happiness and grace in her new post as she did here." She took a step closer to Sister Ursula, "Why are they standing –?"

"I was about to start assigning seats, Mother. Thank you for stopping by. I know how busy the first day of school must be for you."

"Every day is a busy day here at O.L.P.S.! Isn't that right, girls?" Mother pumped a stubby fist in the air, milking enthusiasm from thirty-eight listless girls aching to sit down.

"Yes, Mother!" we shouted in unison.

"Very well, then," Mother gave a nod to us, then to Sister, "have a good morning."

She took two steps toward the door, then quickly did an about-face back and addressed us.

"Ah! One other thing, girls! You will be going into Sister Michael Mary's room in the afternoons for instruction in arithmetic and grammar." Linda's hand shot up. Mother pretended not to see it.

"And the boys will be coming into your room for –" Mother turned to Sister Ursula, "What is it you'll be teaching, Sister?" A hint of our new teacher's previous look of disgust colored her face for a quick second. It was slightly scary seeing it up close, yet she was even more beautiful from this perspective. Sister took a deep breath before responding with an even lower pitched voice, stretching out each syllable, emphasizing every 'T'.

"Literature, American history, health, art –"

"Art? I don't remember any discussion –" Mother stopped herself, looked around at our gawking faces then turned back to Sister, "We'll talk about this later. These girls need to sit down before they faint." As she strutted out of the room, she called over her shoulder, "Announcements will be coming as soon as we get the intercom working."

"What really happened to Sister Agnes?" was the topic of whispers and low talk as we peeled our sweaty backs from the walls, using our knees to keep our stacks of books from cascading, causing our shoulder bags to slip down our arms and collide with the books or our neighbor's shoulder bag, "I bet she got married!"

"And had a baby?"

"She's too smart for that."

"That's why she left the convent."

"And turned into a hippie!"

"She's too old for that."

A few taps on the desk bell brought us to attention. Sister Ursula was standing in front of the room, in profile, still as a statue, looking the defiant martyr. Her entire upper body was tilting upwards, perhaps towards heaven. When the room was silent, she straightened her spine and faced us.

"Could you please arrange yourselves in order by height, the shortest starting at the front door, the tallest over by the window, as quickly and quietly as you possibly can?"

This was something different. Like a musical chair game without the chairs and the music, just the urgency. Christine Livingston took charge, which was her nature and no one bothered to argue. We just wanted to sit down already. After three months of prancing around in bathing suits and shorts, our bodies were suffocating under the wool of our jumpers and knee socks. My feet were not ready to be confined in a closed shoe, even a fashionable pair of penny loafers that were transforming into harbors of angry crowded toes twisting and curling, striving for space or an exit.

Sister pointed at us as she assigned desks, shortest girls in the front row, tallest in the back. This made sense to me. I was smack dab in the middle of the room, with Linda Warner on my right, Angela Andreoli in front of me with her collection of metal barrettes holding her cowlicky hair in place, and Christine Livingston, who smelled like she bathed in a river of orchids, on my left.

My closest friend, Shelly Evans, was in the front row next to the window. I was sad not to be sitting next to her, but thought it a good thing that she was near a window, so she could feel the breeze and watch the seasons change through the huge maples that lined the side of the school building. In the past year, whenever I walked by her house, the curtains were always drawn. As these thoughts were passing through my head, Shelly turned around, and finally, we caught each other's eye, and she smiled at me.

The one other person whose whereabouts in the classroom concerned me was Ellen Boyle. The Boyle family did not bathe with regularity. They lived in the last standing farm house of the pre-World War II days in Cloverdale, when the land was fertile with corn fields and apple trees. It was a one-floor wooden shack of a building hidden behind a development of homes that were built in the early 1950s. Rumor had it that the Boyles did not have running water. Although today it looked as though Ellen had spent the summer washing. Her short brown hair shined and curled softly around her wide moon face which looked rosy and sun-kissed. Her white blouse was crisp with the packaging folds; the pleats of her jumper neatly ironed; the regulation navy socks aligned directly below her knees and her saddle shoes were polished with new laces. In spite of these efforts, it seemed Sister Ursula had been tipped off about the Boyles and placed Ellen in the last seat of the last row by the window.

After settling into our desks, placing books underneath, pens and pencils in the little dip on the desk top, we sat and looked up at our teacher, waiting for her next direction.

"As I call your name please stand and then immediately be seated." She read the roster of names which were in alphabetical order. Afterwards she said, "I shall do my best to learn all your names by the end of the week. I did not expect for there to be so many of you." Again, Linda raised her hand. Sister gave her a cold hard stare. Anyone else would have lowered their arm.

"Is this an urgent question?" Sister asked without moving a facial muscle.

"No, I was just wondering if you were from England. That's all."

"Why on earth would you ask such a question?"

"The way you talk. It's different." Linda gave a shrug and a bit of a snort laugh. I felt embarrassed for Linda, which was a waste of emotion because nothing could embarrass her. I thought she should be more self-conscious. Linda thought I was too self-conscious. She had an older sister with Down-syndrome who I had thought at first was her twin – just a little messier and uncoordinated. Linda didn't seem the least bit hurt by that mistake, she just shrugged and snorted, "Yeah, lots of people think that at first."

Sister was looking at Linda as if she were something she had discovered on the bottom of her shoe. Linda smiled back. Sister looked away from Linda and addressed her answer to the entire room.

"If you must know, I am from Rosemont, a suburb of the Main Line of Philadelphia. However, this is none of your concern, so let us get on with our day and put any questions you may have away until the end of the week, when we will address them together. I may have a few queries myself. Agreed?"

"Yes, Sister!" we answered with a bit more enthusiasm than usual, thinking something exotic was in store for us with this alluring and callous new teacher.

Sister Michael Mary, the seventh-grade boys' teacher, had been at the school for as long as anyone could remember and was clearly the best choice for a mob of prepubescent gangsters. She looked like Steve

105

McQueen and moved like she was manning a Harley. Her body was stocky, but strong. She was also the choir director, played the organ at every Mass and ceremony, and gave piano lessons after school and on weekends. Sister Michael was in a state of perpetual motion. When you were in her presence, you did what was right because you wanted to. She inspired respect.

In the short block of time between recess and going into Sister Michael's room, we had 'health' class, which was a course of Sister Ursula's creation. It was basically a 'how to' on cleanliness and diary-keeping. On the second Friday in September, she instructed us to "jot down any changes we may have noticed in our bodies over the past year." We looked up at her, befuddled.

"Don't think too hard about it. If there were changes you wouldn't have to. Just write."

Walking home later that day with Linda and Shelly I was hoping one of them would bring up the subject of body changes. But it was a Monkees night, so as usual we talked about our favorite Monkee, what song we hoped they'd sing, what crazy trouble they might get into. For that ten-minute walk I forgot about my body.

One change on Linda was obvious. When she stood sideways it looked like she had an end half of a loaf of rye bread tacked to her chest. I thought of asking her when and how that happened but didn't want to do it in front of Shelly. That was a subject for a private conversation. I knew Linda wouldn't mind me asking. She was so good-natured about everything. I wondered how she got that way and if it was something she could teach me to be.

The only change I saw in myself besides getting a little taller and my shoe size going up a half size a year since fifth grade, was hair on my forearms and calves. It wasn't the soft golden downy kind that

Christine Livingston or other blonde girls had. It was the black wiry kind similar to what was on my older brother's arms. I was too horrified and ashamed to talk to anyone about it.

That night, when I was about to step into the bathtub, I noticed another sprout of hair growth between my legs. When did that happen? Overnight? Or had I just not been looking? I had had glimpses of my mother's dark triangle between her legs, so I knew this was not abnormal, it just seemed – too soon. My eyebrows were also threatening to join forces in carpeting the bottom ledge of my forehead.

If I just stayed covered up and ignored these areas of my body, I could pretend that all was normal and fine within me and get through the school year and my time under this nun's coldhearted tutelage. I filled my diary with stories about my disproportionally long legs and big feet and how I coped with their incessant growth.

The last Friday in September was a very unusual seventy-seven degrees and the seventh-grade girls had all played hard at recess. We jumped rope, played Break the Golden Gate with the eighth-grade girls, and some of us let ourselves be spirited around the playground by our hormones, running after and from any sixth-to eighth-grade boy brave enough to talk to us.

At 1:05 we sprinted and stumbled up to the third floor sweaty, giddy, and out of breath. Sister Ursula stood three steps from the staircase, guarding the back door with her daunting icy clean figure. Normally we would just burst into the classroom on our own accord, using both the back and front doors and go to our desks. Sister would be at the board writing or at her desk, paying little attention to our return. Sometimes she wasn't even in the room. We considered these five to ten minutes after recess as our own cool down time. We'd continue talking, although in softer voices, get a drink, go to the bathroom, take care of our after-lunch needs. It was a transition time from silliness to stillness.

Today, Sister Ursula was standing against the door, forcing us to squeeze by her in the most graceful way possible, so as not to contaminate her with our sweaty bodies. After we all had taken our seats, she marched to the front of the room, turned to us with a flourish and hissed:

"Do I have to get into the shower with each and every one of you and show you how to clean yourself?"

A picture immediately flashed into my head of Sister Ursula, her tall statuesque frame, naked and pearly white, sitting in our avocado green bathtub. She would surely be disgusted with my family's shower-less – 'stuck-in-the-50s'- bathroom. I could feel my face reddening with shame.

As if she could hear my thoughts, she continued, "Sit-down baths are unsanitary, as you are merely soaking in a pool of your own filth." She was walking up and down the aisles, her arms tucked inside her sleeves, her nostrils expanding and contracting. I held my breath as she walked by my desk and didn't completely exhale until she was out of my peripheral vision. The room went silent and still for a few seconds, followed by a murmur of voices, another silence, the sound of a chair moving, soft footsteps, the back door opening, then quickly closing. Sister appeared in the front of the room.

"Everyone: Raise your hand!" We all complied while Sister looked at us with a smug smile. I took a quick glance at the back of the room and as I suspected, Ellen's desk was empty.

"Now turn your head towards your raised arm and sniff, deeply." I didn't know whether to laugh or cry. This attention to our bodies was approaching humiliation. Sister was holding up a huge can of 'Right Guard' deodorant.

"Fetid," she snarled, "putrid 'baby powder' is what I smell up here. Young ladies, 'baby powder' is for, as it is rightly named – BABIES. Not for growing and some fully grown girls such as yourselves. You all need deodorant, some more than others. This product will be on the back shelf in the cloak closet next to a box of disposable sanitary napkins." She slammed the can down on the desk.

"Raise your hand if you have started menstruating."

My heart began pounding into my ears as a faint sizzle resonated in my head. I dropped my focus to the meshy wood of my desktop, hoping to lose myself in the maze of ink and carvings. I was still wearing an undershirt and had no understanding of menstruation other than it involved frequent and solemn trips to the girls' room throughout the day with little brown bags.

I missed the movie they showed to the sixth-grade girls that explained all you needed to know about becoming a lady. It was the only day of the whole school year I was out, and I wasn't even sick. My mother had made me stay home and she had yet to keep her promise and explain the 'facts of life' to me.

A fortress of single arms rose up around me like freshly drawn swords. I couldn't lift my eyes to see if Shelly had her hand raised. How could I go on if she did? I needed her and me to be in the same place. Time had stopped. When was this witch of a nun going to let them put their hands down? Was she counting them?

"Twenty-eight. That's nearly three-fourths."

Whew! I wasn't alone. Was Shelly one of those nine?

"When you are in your 'monthly', lower your arms please, you should change your pad at least every hour, no matter the day or the amount of flow. Every hour, even if it is less than a tablespoon, you should still change it. In the meantime, I ask all of you to keep each other in check on body odor and other –"

There was a knock on the front door, quickly followed by the entrance of Sister Michael with her arm around a mortified Ellen Boyle, whose head was bowed so deeply you could see the back of her grimy neck. It was evident that Ellen had had limited access to water since school had begun a month ago. Her uniform was wrinkled, her blouse sepia-toned and she was enveloped in a waft of fecal matter and cheese that was hard to ignore.

"This child was standing in the hallway –"

"She was instructed to go to the lavatory and wash –"

"– CRYING!" Sister Michael bellowed that last word with her powerful tenor, which could silence a battlefield. The nuns were standing on either side of Ellen, who was curling deeper into herself, trying to disappear. Sister Ursula brought her hand dramatically to her nose and took a step backwards.

"Clearly, Ellen, you have not followed instructions." Ellen's neck and face flushed chili-red as she fled out of the room. Sister Michael looked like she was about to punch Sister Ursula, who shifted her body out of the line of Sister Michael's fire and quipped, "She is a health hazard."

A wave of nervous giggles coursed through the aisles which Sister Michael acknowledged with a frown. She then eyed the huge can of Right Guard and turned her focus to the room. "Where is Mary? Mary Lanza? Oh! There you are, Dear, right under my nose!"

Mary Lanza was the one person who related to Ellen in a normal way. She would walk with her to and from school, talking in what looked like a natural, relaxed manner. They may have lived near each other, or perhaps Ellen had lunch at Mary's house. She was a tiny, dark-haired, elfin-like girl with large almond-shaped brown eyes and a thin triangle of a mouth that never lost its shape, even when she spoke.

"I'm going to borrow Mary for a short while, Sister. We'll hold off on changing classes for thirty minutes." Sister Michael started towards the door with her arm gently around her as it had been around Ellen minutes ago. "Make it an hour," she called over her shoulder. Once out the door she turned and said, "I'll send a boy over to tell you when." With that, Sister Michael and Mary disappeared into the hallway. Ursula's creamy complexion was churning into a frosty strawberry. She marched back to her desk, slammed open a drawer, pulled out a can of Lysol, and then sprayed the area where Ellen and Sister Michael had stood, tracing the outline of their figures.

"I want you girls to write a list of all the products you use to clean yourself. Tell me how you use it, how many times a day and when. This was an unpleasant occurrence for everyone. Let's not have it happen again."

Linda's hand shot up. Sister quickly turned her back. That didn't stop Linda from calling out.

"But Sister –"

"There will be no discussion on this matter."

Christine Livingston came to Linda's defense, "She doesn't have water, Sister."

"That is neither mine nor your problem, Christine. All you or I can do for her is set an example. Continue working in silence until one of Sister Michael's boys comes with a message." She spewed the last part of the sentence, like she was saying something dirty.

When we went into Sister Michael's classroom seventy-five minutes later, Mary and Ellen were already seated in the center of the room, writing in their notebooks. Ellen had on a clean white blouse and black skirt. Her hair was damp, her face calm and glowing. She was sitting upright, her head gently tilted towards her right shoulder, a hint of a smile on her face as she focused on her notebook, her left hand moving gracefully across the page.

Mary had hooked her hair behind her ears, which were large for her head. This slight adjustment gave her an overall pointy and other-worldly appearance. She seemed a tad older and wiser, as if she had been on a journey or taken part in a ritual of a foreign country. Sister Michael was at the board, whistling and bouncing, diagramming an elaborate sentence from Life magazine. There was a scent of Ivory soap and Breck shampoo in the air.

We entered the room with tentativeness – slowly and mindful of our footing as if we were going to the altar to receive Communion. But this was more than ceremony. There was mysticism in the air! A living circuit of light was coursing between these three females. As I sat down at my desk, I felt a strange fluttering in my ribcage, which I could only identify as a cleansing in my soul brought on by the exposure to the holy joyousness in the room. It was evident that something magical and powerful had transpired. However, what actually did take place was simple: Sister Michael had taken Ellen to the convent for a shower and a change into clean clothes. Mary helped.

But that was never stated or discussed, so we all made up our own version of the event. It was the unknown, the unwritten chapter we filled in with what we surmised and pictured happening – nakedness, water, showering in a sacred place – and everything in between, before the ending, where Ellen was clean and Sister Ursula had soiled her own allure.

A Race for Redemption

Father Tillman decided at the last minute to have our track team show in the 440 Yard Race and put me in fourth position – anchor. I was in the seventh grade, on the second string of Our Lady of Perpetual Sorrow's girl's 1968 Track Team. The event was to be held at Kennedy Stadium in Philadelphia. He had not trained us for a 440 run, but when he called my name, I was honored and terrified. Saying 'no' was not an option.

It felt like I was going to my execution as I took my place behind the white line on the third lane track with hundreds of people in the stands watching and yelling contradictory instructions. I was smack dab in the middle of eight runners who towered over me and had large substantial feet clad in black and red high-top Converse sneakers.

These girls could not possibly have been seventh or eighth graders unless they had been held back for five years. They all seemed to know one another or just hated each other on sight and were comfortable saying so. I was catching words such as: "bitch, nigger, pig" along with verbs like "dare, kill, knock you out" and others I didn't recognize or knew how to spell. In my world even the hint of an utterance of any of these words would get you a smack across the face.

This was nothing like the 220-yard race I had run under an hour ago, where everyone was so nice. The winning team of very tall blonde girls who looked like they just walked off the set of My Three Sons wished us all luck. It wasn't hard to share in their victory because they made us feel good and confident, and grateful to be involved. I decided to try to recreate that happy, positive atmosphere.

The runner on my left was fidgeting with her red high-top, kneeling on one leg with the other bent. In this position we were almost head-to-head, so when I caught her eye, I smiled. My rival froze, gripped her laces like she was riding a wild horse, and glared at me with such intensity I thought she was either counting my freckles or trying to figure out when and where I had pissed her off. After about ten seconds, a wide Chiclet grin ripped across her face and without breaking eye contact, yanked her laces, let loose a spray of spit over her left shoulder and shouted across the lanes, "Hey, Darby! Hey, you bitch in that last lane! I got something to say to you!"

Relieved to not be Darby, I quickly returned my focus back to myself and then to the girl on my right to see if she had witnessed any of that bizarre moment so that we could roll our eyes in unison and sigh with understanding and camaraderie.

This girl was in the middle of a runner's stretch and simultaneously cracking her knuckles. Her eyes were shooting daggers to the top of the bleachers as her right foot nonchalantly slid forward, landing her in a full split. Her legs reminded me of the furniture in my grandmother's house – a silky shiny mahogany, sheathing a myriad of muscled curves. From foot to foot, she was about two and a half yards long. After snapping and popping all ten fingers, she raised both arms (each the length and girth of my legs) in a defiant two-handed finger to the entire stadium. I started a rosary in my head.

114

The moment the starter gun fired the other anchors intensified their stretching. I tried to copy their movements. Stretching was not part of Father Tilman's training and these girls looked like professional runners to me. Once their third position gained on them, they held out their right arm, their bodies and feet facing forward, their heads almost fully rotated over their backs screaming profane incentives to their teammate.

No, a rosary would not be enough. I began a novena. "O Most Blessed Mother..." That's all I could remember. I went back to the rosary.

As soon as I grabbed my baton and started to take off with my right leg leading, something caught my left ankle, causing me to trip and stumble. I didn't fall, but I lost precious seconds our team needed to keep its place in the front four. That something was the knuckle-cracking, bird-flipping runner's left foot. There was no time to feel defiant or hurt or to try to figure out why she did that. We had never even made eye contact. It did occur to me that perhaps she could read minds and caught my comparison of her legs to my grandmother's furniture.

The race was torturous, twice the length of the race I had run only an hour ago. There was no end to the black glittering asphalt as it bent and curved along and between the white lines that separated me from the other girls. It took all my will power to keep myself upright and in motion. One reel in my brain was reciting Hail Mary's while the other tried to make out what Father Tillman was shouting at me. His was the one voice out of hundreds that I heard and continued to hear in my head throughout the race. I was the sixth runner to cross the line. Darby was the first. That's all I learned.

My team was already heading towards the parking lot as I walked
– heavy and drenched with sweat, failure, and shame – off the field. I
filed in with the swarm of people several yards behind and started
towards the gate, still trying to catch my breath.

"You should have kicked that nigger in the shins!" Father Tillman
had emerged from the crowd and was now cornering me against a trash
bin. His lips curled tightly over his gums, exposing a mouthful of mossy
coated teeth.

"What's the matter with you?" He hissed. His face was chafed and
ruddy with fury and sunburn. He edged in closer overwhelming me
with a gust of frankincense and sweat radiating from his gloomy
cassock.

"That dirty nigger tripped you! And you stupid – you shoulda
kicked that goddamn nigger's ass!" My heart started throbbing in my
ears. Mrs. Antonelli, one of the chaperone moms appeared at his side
and began coaxing him away from me. At the same time Mrs.
Cavanaugh, another chaperone mom, grabbed my arm and pulled me
towards the nearest exit. The space between me and the priest expanded
and began filling with runners, coaches, spectators, but I could still hear
him ranting, "That nigger should be disqualified!"

According to every adult in Our Lady of Perpetual Sorrow's parish,
Father Tillman was the closest human being to God in a two-mile
radius. He was our direct connection to the Lord; the person you
confessed all your nasty secrets and sins to; the person who bestowed
God's forgiveness upon you, assuring you an eternity of happiness and
purity in heaven; the person whose judgment trumped everyone else's
in the community.

That brought into question for me: What kind of God would grant sanctity to someone who referred to another race of people with a forbidden word? Use of that word indicated that you considered this person less than human. I was about to put all these thoughts into a question for Mrs. Cavanaugh when she suddenly spun around, knelt on the gravel drive, grabbed hold of my upper arms and said, "You are NOT to talk about this with any of the other girls. Do you understand?"

I wasn't sure if she was pleading with me or commanding me, so I was feeling sorry for her at the same time she frightened me. "Do you?" Mrs. Cavanaugh's eyebrows connected into a 'V' above her eyes as she squeezed my arms. I wanted to sit down already, so I peeled my tongue off the roof of my mouth and said in a raspy whisper, "Okay."

That seemed to satisfy Mrs. Cavanaugh and we headed towards the grayish white Volkswagen bus, where the eleven other runners were filing into the back, like prisoners, taking a seat on the floor. Mrs. Hoffman, the third chaperone mom, was at the wheel. I stumbled into the back and Mrs. Cavanaugh took the front passenger seat next to Mrs. Hoffman. As we were making our way out of the parking lot, the vehicle came to a sudden halt and Mrs. Cavanaugh opened the door to a panting Mrs. Antonelli, who climbed in and onto Mrs. Cavanaugh's lap. There was an indecipherable conversation amongst the three women, probably having to do with why Mrs. Antonelli was carrying her black patent leather strappy shoes and why she was not riding back with Father Tillman since she had ridden to the stadium with him.

Once we made it onto the expressway and my heart started beating normally, my last Confession with Father Tillman flashed in my head, and I shuddered with shame. After what I just experienced with him, two questions came to mind: Did that last Confession 'take' with God? More importantly, was his treatment of me in any way related to what I confessed to him? It was common knowledge that he made it a point to know who was in his Confession box. There were a couple of times I allowed my eyes to look forward only to be pierced by two teal-blue orbs glaring behind the dark screen.

I looked around the dusty bus at the other girls. What were they thinking? Someone must have heard his ranting. I couldn't make out what anyone was saying. Gertrude Pitelli was showing a group of eighth graders a hand clapping game with some dirty words. The rest were laughing and chatting like it was just another day. Nobody seemed to care about the outcome of the 440 race. The other three girls that ran it weren't even sitting with each other.

I needed a friend. The only person I was ever really close and personal with was Shelly Evans and she wasn't here. These girls were strangers, except for Dotty Elliot, who had lent me her dickey. Her back yard was right across from mine, separated by a white ranch-style fence. She had three equally beautiful sisters, all smart, slender brunettes of varying degrees of prettiness and height, ages 10 – 16, each two years apart. They all played the piano, read above their grade level, and collected model horses.

Two years ago, they had moved from a large single home on the opulent side of the boulevard to our block of twin homes, because Mr. Eliot had died suddenly from a heart attack. My mother said, "He was a very kind man," and that "he looked like Gregory Peck." This fact only added to my adoration of this tragic storybook family. I could never be totally myself around these girls. I had to be better.

Dotty was waving and calling to me. Maybe I could tell her what happened? She had gone through a terrible tragedy. She would be sensitive to my feelings. Dotty's lips were moving but I couldn't hear her over the other girls' squealing, which was growing louder.

"What are you saying? I can't hear you!"

"Can I have my dickey back?"

"What?"

"My dickey! The collar I lent you!"

"I took it off!"

"Where is it?"

"It was too hot."

"Where did you put it?"

I reached into my front pocket. I had absentmindedly ripped the collar off at the end of the race and stuck it in my right pocket. I didn't remember exactly how I got it off my white V-neck sweater. Were there snaps or buttons? I was upright on my knees, digging into my empty right pocket.

"What are you doing to yourself Cassie?" Somebody called out in a judgmental tone which I chose to ignore.

I pulled my right hand out of my pocket as I rummaged through the left pocket with my left hand. Nothing. I looked apologetically at Dotty, but she was now caught in the tumble of girls on the other side of the bus, lying on her side, comparing medals with Nora Dougherty, which I thought was pointless because we all got a standard medal for participating.

I started groping around on the floor. It must have fallen out somehow.

"Watcha looking for?"

I pretended I didn't hear that voice again. That mean sarcastic 'looking for trouble tenor' that came from Ronnie Shriver, the self-appointed captain of the team. She was close to six feet, with a thick, short flaxen mane that she wore greased back off her face. Everything about her was angular and strong. She would make a very attractive boy that I might like if it were so. But it wasn't so and I had an aversion to her and she knew it and did her best to provoke me. She was probably the reason I had to run in that horrible race, which she ran in first position. It was obvious that she blamed me for the team's loss by the way she was taunting me.

"You need some help?" She was now kneeling in front of me. I was eye level with her ribs.

"No," I looked up at her with squinted eyes. I was trying to look dangerous.

She grabbed my right pocket open with one hand as she dug with the other, then just as quickly and forcefully yanked her hand out, causing me to slip forward and hit my face against her flat hard damp chest, before falling backwards.

"What did you lose?" Nora asked. She and Dotty were tapping their medals together, pretending they were kissing or something.

"Dotty's dickey."

"Dotty! You have a dickey?" Nora started tickling Dotty. "Let me see it! You gotta let me see your dickey!" They were hysterically hysterical rolling into a lower body embrace, their upper bodies acting unaware, downplaying the pleasure they were both feeling as their pelvises pressed into each other.

"You won't find a dickey there!" Janice Hoffman howled when I accidently poked her in the crotch. The van shook with hilarity. I was praying it would career off the freeway into a ditch and explode. Maybe it would now that Father Tillman had blasphemed himself.

"What's so funny about a dickey?" I asked.

"She doesn't know what a dickey is!" Ronnie informed the entire bus.

Looking at Ronnie's two-pocketed backside I remembered that I also had a two-pocketed backside. I reached my hand into my right pocket and there it was! Dotty's dickey! I held it up in victory.

"I found it!" I cheered.

"Where was it?" Dotty asked.

"I was sitting on it." Success! Relief swept through my upper body as I basked in this small triumph. Father Tillman, his mossy mouth spewing racial slurs, and the oversized scary mean girls, receded further into the past.

"You were sitting on Dotty's dickey!" Ronnie announced to the bus. Screams, shouts, wails of cruel laughter rocked the van so violently I thought it was going to roll off the road. Mrs. Cavanaugh turned around, knocking Mrs. Antonelli onto the gear shift, and lambasted us with threats, dares, and recriminations. Why she hadn't shut them up sooner was just spiteful to me. One theory I had was that she knew that I thought she might be part man – she had a pronounced Adam's apple and had to stoop whenever she went through a doorway. I never said that aloud to anyone, but maybe there was a look on my face that said that to her. After a few minutes of quiet, I whispered to Dotty who was now sitting right across from me.

"Dotty, can you tell me what's so funny –?"

"No. I can't!" She whispered. "I can't tell you. I wish I could but I can't. And don't ask me again." We rode the last ten minutes of the thirty-minute ride in silence.

Some girls even fell asleep. I envied them.

As soon as the van pulled into the rectory driveway and the motor had stopped, I pushed the back door open and fled. Last one in, first out. Once I stepped onto the blacktop, my knees buckled. It felt as if my feet were preventing my legs from realizing their newfound length. I did my best to widen the separation between myself and the rest of the team by walking as fast as my wobbly self could take me out of the rectory area, around the church and onto Jackson Avenue.

Our Country Squire station wagon was parked across the street from the church, where my mother stood talking with Mrs. Eliot, a few feet apart from a circle of other track team moms. My mother was just as enchanted with the Eliot family as I was. Marie Eliot was a model of refinement and courage, but more importantly for my mother, she signified independence and status – two things my mother coveted. Our oval of houses was too blue-collar for my mother, and she had trouble maintaining friendships with the other housewives for any length of time. She cultivated her relationship with Mrs. Eliot through exchanging C.S. Lewis books, classical music records, and having lengthy discussions about Jackie Kennedy's future and their thoughts on Vatican II.

"Did you give Dotty back her dickey?" Were the first words out of her mouth as soon as she set eyes on me.

"Yes!" I wailed.

"What's the matter with you? Did you come in last?"

I wasn't going to even acknowledge that mean spirited question. I stomped across the street to our station wagon, hoping to have a few moments of privacy, only to discover my nine-year old brother Freddy in the front seat rolling a tiny Matchbox bulldozer over the dashboard. I dove into the back and watched from a safe distance the mayhem that occurred as the track team caught up and merged with the mothers, forming a huge noisy swarm as mothers and daughters shouted their conversations over the din of the other exchanges.

Once Mrs. Cavanaugh entered the mob, all heads turned toward her and the action froze as she barked orders and motioned with her arms, one saying 'go away' and the other 'stay put and come closer'. She then folded her arms across her chest and watched as her directions were carried out and the girls scattered away to their cars or homes and the mothers formed a small circle around her. I sunk down in the back seat so as not to be seen by Ronnie and some of the others as they passed in front and around our car.

"Ronald." Freddy muttered as Ronnie passed his window. He turned around on his knees and rolled his bulldozer over the top of his bucket seat with accompanying sound effects.

"Are they gone?" I asked.

"Why're you hiding?"

"Is the coast clear?" My neck was starting to hurt and I wanted to sit up and check on the moms. He stuck his head out the window and looked up and down the street.

"Mister Cavanaugh!" My brother giggled wickedly. We had talked about the questionable gender of this giant lady several times.

"Forget it!" I sat up slightly, peeked out the window, and caught my mother and Mrs. Eliot leaving the circle of ladies while Mrs. Cavanaugh was still holding court.

Mrs. Eliot was holding my mother's arm as they slowly crossed the street together. My mother's face looked pained and confused. Mrs. Eliot looked taller and fuller than my mother. They seemed to be finishing a conversation as they approached the car. I sat back into the seat, wishing it would absorb me into its leathery comfort.

"How are you, Cassie?" Mrs. Eliot's stoic and saintly face appeared in the window.

"You never said hello to Mrs. Eliot." My mother's face joined hers. She looked younger and prettier than Mrs. Eliot. The Eliot girls must have gotten their good looks from their father, I thought. Then I felt guilty about that thought and said a quick Act of Contrition.

"How many times have I told you not to play with that thing on the car seats!"

"I wasn't." Freddy turned and glumly sat forward in his seat.

"Hello, Freddy." Mrs. Eliot was gazing at Freddy with sheer joy. Four kids and all girls. Was that what killed Mr. Eliot? Where were these thoughts coming from?

123

"Hi!" Freddy quickly responded to Mrs. Eliot's loving nature.

"I'll call you later, Marie." My mother was now at the wheel. "Thank you."

"God bless, Betty." She watched as we drove away and turned the corner.

"Somebody tripped you?" My mother addressed the rearview mirror.

"Who told you that?"

"What does it matter who told me? You must be hungry."

"Thirsty." For the first time in hours my body seemed to be wanting attention. My mouth and throat were parched.

"Don't tell me you haven't had anything to drink!"

"I don't know."

"What do you mean you don't know? You don't know if you had a drink?"

"I don't remember! What else did she say?"

"What else did who say?" We were turning onto our street. The ride was at the most two minutes even under the worst of circumstances.

"Mister Cavanaugh," Freddy sneaked up on his knees and giggled. My mother smacked him on the butt.

"Sit down before you go through the windshield!" Freddy plopped back down.

"Did they tell you what Father Tillman said?"

"Wha'd he say?" My little brother was up on his knees again. "He said that word?"

"How do you know about that?" I wailed.

"I TOLD YOU TO SIT DOWN!" My mother didn't even brake when she turned into the driveway. Luckily Freddy was sitting when she did step on it. All was quiet while my mother put the car in park and turned off the engine.

124

"What word?" She asked.

"He hates colored people," Freddy exclaimed with repulsion and awe to the dashboard. My mother pulled the keys out of the ignition like an after-thought. It was early June, the sun still high in the sky at 7:00PM. This was my mother's favorite time of year, her threshold for happiness limitless. It seemed like that threshold had been swallowed up in my little brother's remark.

"He does so much for you children," she said to the windshield.

Freddy leaned over and kissed her on the cheek.

"It's okay, Mommy."

A slight smile flashed on my mother's face as she turned to my brother and lovingly brushed her hand over his ginger buzz cut.

"Go get ready for bed."

As I watched Freddy scramble out of the car, up the drive and into the backyard, my mother leaned against her door and turned to me, pointing her right index finger.

"Cassie, you are not to mention any of this to your sister."

Again, an adult was ordering me to forget. How else could I keep my mouth shut about this?

"Why?"

"Just do as I say."

"What does it matter? Patty doesn't even go to church anymore. She said she's not a Catholic!" Patty was three years older than me and now a sophomore at St. Bernadette's Girls Academy. When she was in eighth-grade she spent her Sundays at the rectory counting the collection money for Father Tillman.

"Listen to me, Father Tillman is a good man."

"He called me stupid –"

"He doesn't mean anything with what he says. We shouldn't think badly of him."

"For not kicking the girl in the shins! He said I shoulda kicked her in the shins! And called her that word!"

My mother gathered her keys and pocketbook and opened the car door and stepped out.

"Enough. Come on. You need to drink something." She was holding my door open, waiting for me.

"You'll dehydrate sitting there any longer."

"Will not."

I didn't really know what she meant by that, but I wasn't going to immediately believe anything my mother said from that day forward.

My sister was standing in the middle of the kitchen with one fist in a water glass, drying it with a red-checkered dish cloth.

"I heard. He's a racist bigot like I always said."

My mother stepped between my sister and me and threateningly pointed her finger in her face. "Do not use that language in this house young lady!"

Patty stepped into my mother's finger and looked her dead in the eye, "Why? Those words are in the dictionary."

My mother had no answer or didn't think my sister worthy of a discourse. She took a glass off the dishrack, turned on the spigot, and when it was full, handed it to me.

"Drink. They didn't stop and let them get a drink," she said to nobody in particular. My father appeared in the doorway, a rolled-up newspaper in his hand.

"After all that running!" She shouted at him. "Can you imagine?"

"What are you talking about, Betty?" He went back into the living room, sat in his chair, and opened to the sports page.

My sister stomped in after him. "Father Tillman told Cassie she was stupid for 'not kicking the nigger' for tripping her in the race."

"What's this all about, Betty?"

"I just told you!" Patty stomped both feet, one after the other, like a colt. "You're gonna get a call all about it from Crabby Cavanaugh." She turned to me. "You poked Janice Hoffman in the crotch?"

"It was an accident – I did not!"

"How do you know all this?" My mother asked.

"My friends."

"What friends?"

"Dad! Did you hear what I just said?" Patty screamed.

"Answer your mother." My father went back to the sports page.

"I did!" It looked like Patty was about to put her fist through our father's paper.

"Cassie, come wash your hands and eat your dinner." My mother had put together a plate of cold chicken, iceberg lettuce, carrots, and a lukewarm baked potato.

Patty marched back into the kitchen and slammed the glass, with the dishtowel still in it, onto the kitchen counter. She then stomped out of the kitchen, through the living room and up the stairs, causing the house to vibrate with her fury. My father lowered his paper.

"What's all the commotion?"

My mother sighed and removed the dishtowel from the glass.

Fifteen minutes later I was pounding on my bedroom door. The Rolling Stones were belting on the other side: "... it's just a shot away. War! Children...!" My sister and I hated this arrangement. We'd been roommates since Freddy was three. We were supposed to get our own rooms two years ago but my parents never got around to it. Our only recourse was to lock each other out every now and then.

"LET ME IN! I'm gonna tell Mom!"

The doorknob gave a little heave and a turn. My sister had

mastered turning the flimsy lock with such a subtlety – not a sound and barely visible. Once I was standing outside for about ten minutes before realizing she had unlocked it.

Patty was at the mirror painting her eyelids violet blue. I stepped around her, belly flopped onto my bed, and buried my face in the pillow. If only I could die for a day or so and come back to life once everybody had forgotten about today. I started imagining what it would be like to be temporarily dead when my sister's bossy voice interrupted my thinking.

"You've got B.O."

"You've got B.O!"

"It's okay if you have B.O!"

"NO IT'S NOT!"

"You were running! Get over it and grow up!"

She ran a brush through her hair, then slammed out of the room.

Two hours later, when I was under the covers and just about to slip into sleep, the ceiling light flicked on. I sat up in alarm only to see Patty locking the door. She had the same clothes on – a shades of gray checkered shorts set. She seemed to have a friend in checkers. Everything about her was opposites; the type of opposites that made a pattern.

"Where were you?" I asked.

"He pushed Mrs. Antonelli out of the car. Called her a nosey Wop."

That wasn't an answer, but it was information – important information. Patty started to change into her pajamas. I turned my head to give her privacy. That was the rule. Never watch anyone take their clothes off.

"Did she call the police? How do you know this?"

"I don't know and I heard it from Janice, who heard it from Joey

Hoffman, who heard it from either his sister who you poked, or his mother who was, as you know, a chaperone. Why aren't you asleep?"

"You woke me up. Is she going to do anything about it?"

"Who?"

"Mrs. Antonelli!"

"What should she do?"

"Call the police? Or the Archdiocese? There's gotta be a law or commandment about pushing ladies and telling kids to fight and calling them stupid! Don't you think?"

"Of course I do."

"And using that word!"

I thought Patty would say more, but she turned off the light and got into bed.

"Then..." I wasn't sure what to say. Why don't you do something? Or, let's do something, you and me! Or... I looked over at Patty and she was fast asleep, her mouth slightly open, her lips pale and dry, her black hair wild and loose on the pillow. If a stranger walked into this room right now, I thought, they would probably look at her and smile, and then look at me and wonder why I wasn't asleep.

The Primrose Path

It all started with my mother's tuna casserole. I ate too much, became violently ill, and consequently bed ridden, for two days. I was thirteen and shared a periwinkle-blue bedroom with my messy sixteen-year-old sister Patty, who was now bent over brushing the underside of her hair. She continued brushing while uncurling her body into a straight standing position. Her hair now looked full and luscious. My sister was cutting edge! Why couldn't I be more like her? She caught my eye in the mirror and sneered, "You really pigged out on that tuna casserole, didn't you?"

"Shut up." I was in no mood. I was bored and dying of thirst. My mother was not taking any chances with me not making it to the bathroom again. She was killing me slowly through dehydration.

"I got a really good book if you want something to read." Patty was painting her lips a cotton candy pink. She was the best-looking kid of the four of us and she knew it. Somehow, she was blessed with a normal nose that didn't upstage the rest of her face as my brothers and I had. The one plus I had on her were my long legs, but they came with super big feet that would not stop growing. She was adding a hint of white over the pink on her full-lipped perfect mouth. I hated watching her make herself even better looking, but I had nothing else to do and I had already slept sixteen hours.

"Get lost," I moaned. I didn't mean it, but it was my strategy. I always said the opposite of what I meant to get Patty to do what I wanted. How she hadn't figured this out by now proved to me that I was smarter than her.

"It's really scary." She dumped the entire contents of her shoulder bag onto her bed. A waft of stale tobacco and peppermint drifted into my nostrils and suddenly I was not so thirsty, and my stomach filled with tiny butterflies.

"What's it about?" I pushed myself into a seated position.

"I don't know, I didn't read it –"

"What!" I protested. This was vintage Patty, egging others on to do things she would never do, for her own amusement.

"Don't get dramatic – all my girlfriends did, and they said it was really scary, and they're juniors! So, you know it's not a kiddy book." Patty had dug the dog-eared black–and-red paperback from the pile on her bed and handed it to me.

"Rosemary's Baby?" That didn't sound scary to me. Patty was back at the mirror assessing her face from different angles with a hand mirror.

"Do NOT tell anyone I gave it to you."

"Why?"

"You know..." She pulled down one eyelid at a time and traced a thick black line across the tip to the temple. She was hiding from me. Was she going to finish the sentence, or was she dropping the conversation and hoping I'd let it go?

"Know what? What do I know?" She finally opened her eyes and met mine in the mirror, and with a tortured sigh, turned and faced me.

"Mom! She thinks I'm evil." Her chin was pointing upward as in defiance at the very thought, while her nostrils flared with excitement and her eyes lowered in hurt and shame. And she told me not to get dramatic. I played along.

"Really?" I gulped in fake disbelief.

"Yeah, like I'll lead you down the primrose path or something."

"Where is that? I wanna go!" I squealed in complete earnestness.

"You wanna go down the primrose path?" Patty was squishing her mascara wand in and out of the tube. Her eyes already looked big and stunned.

"Yea!" I was on my knees, bouncing in place.

"Do you even know what a primrose path is?"

Visions flashed in my head of emerald lanes lined with vines of colorful roses leading to turquoise lakes where nymphs and centaurs lounged around on smooth shiny rocks eating grapes and admiring each other and themselves in the watery reflection. A fantasy, a compilation of a Max Parrish painting and a Bible illustration, but maybe something similar existed? And if it did, Patty would know where it was!

"I don't care! I wanna go! I wanna go somewhere! I've never been anywhere or done anything! It's not fair! I do everything I'm told and I never have any fun!" Suddenly I was overtaken by sobs. After a night of vomiting and a day of fasting, this was not unfathomable for a prepubescent thirteen-year-old.

"So emotional." My sister was back at the mirror brushing her eyelashes with the black goo. Who was she doing that for? It was a school night and already eight o'clock.

"Everybody else ate the tuna casserole! Why was I the only one who got sick?" I was squeezing the paperback, endowing it with the power to keep me from hyperventilating or dry heaving. I wanted my sister to stop looking at herself and come hug me. As if she heard my wish, she marched over to my bed, but instead of hugging me, she grabbed the book from my fist with her free hand.

"You have to promise NOT to let Mom see this. And if she does: DO NOT, I REPEAT, DO NOT tell her I gave it to you. Promise?"

Now I really wanted to read this book.

"I promise," I solemnly vowed as I wrenched the paperback from her hand.

I covered the book with brown paper so nobody was the wiser and finished it in twenty-four hours. My sister was right. It wasn't a kiddy book. The characters smoked, drank, held séances and were not exactly nice or honest with each other. But there was one part that I did not understand at all. My plan was to ask Shelly, my closest friend, the next day when I went back to school. Not surprisingly, Shelly was absent. She'd been absent a lot during the year, and it was our last in grade school. I wasn't worried so much because she wasn't sick. She had things to take care of at home, she told me. That's about all she would tell me and I didn't want to pry.

My second choice of confidant was Linda Warner. However, in my two-day absence, Linda had acquired a side-kick – Angela Andreoli, a tense, skinny, sharp-featured girl. I sent Linda a note telling her I had something really important to show her and asked her to meet me on the steps of the old school building at recess. When I got to the steps, Linda was already there with Angela, both engrossed in making a gum-wrapper chain. My heart sank. This was an intimate, best-friend activity! They both looked up. Angela's braces were catching the sunlight causing rays to blaze into my eyes.

"This is kinda private," I said to the two of them while giving Angela a 'get lost' look.

"Why?" Angela asked in her high soprano yelp.

"It just is." I took my spot on the steps.

"It's okay, Cassie. You can tell us both," I looked up at Linda, who was sitting on the top step. Her bulging blue-green eyes were like friendly lakes you wanted to dive into. At thirteen, Linda was inching towards five-feet-eight inches and weighing close to one hundred and forty pounds. Everyone knew that she and her mother shared a wardrobe, which didn't seem to bother her one iota. She was smiling at me with her two crooked front teeth resting on her bottom lip. How could I not trust her? I showed them the book, gave them the back story, and started reading:

"He slipped a hand in under her buttocks, raised them, lodged his hardness against her, and pushed it powerfully in. Bigger he was than always; painfully, wonderfully big. He lay forward –"

That was as far as I got before Angela knocked the book to the ground, screeching, "You better shut up or you're going to go to hell!"

For just reading it? Everything about Angela was alarming – her metal mouth, her steel eyeglasses, her big gold hooped earrings and busy hair with its assortment of shiny barrettes. Maybe she accessorized her head to make up for her tininess? Standing side by side, the two reminded me of Mutt and Jeff – a comic strip that wasn't funny, but that I read anyway.

"No! Let her finish, Angie!" Linda cheered.

"Linda! Don't you know it's a sin? And not just a venial sin! You better go to Confession, Cassie! In case you die!"

This was nonsense. I just wanted clarification on one particular thing and then I'd drop the whole subject. "But, 'lodging his hardness', do you know what that means?"

"Of course, we do!" Angela said with a 'you must be stupid expression'.

"We do?" It looked like this was news to Linda.

"Yeah! We do!" Angela silently mouthed to Linda: PEEE NISSS.

"Oh! Yeah! We do!" Linda answered with a big smile and a couple of snorts. How much ground had these two covered in two days?

"What? What does that mean?"

"It's a secret," Linda answered. "Only your mother can tell you." It looked like Linda was feeling sorry for me, which felt kind of good for a second before Angela stepped right into my face.

"You have to ask her – you have to ask her about THE FACTS OF LIFE." Angela's breath smelled like nasty moth balls. "And she HAS to tell you. It's her duty as a mother."

How was I going to ask my mother about this without her finding out about the book?

Linda continued, "And you can't laugh or get scared. And after she tells you – you can't tell anybody! You should just forget about the whole thing until you get married."

What a strange thing to do with information – gather, process, and put away.

"But before you ask her," Angela interrupted my thought, "you have to ask yourself: ARE YOU READY?" she shouted at my face, like she was at an Eagles game. She paused a moment and looked me up and down with her pointy nose, "You know, Cassie, you really should be. I mean, you're almost in high school. I can't believe your mother hasn't told you before."

What was my mother doing to me? Why was she torturing me into ignorance? She had kept me home from school in sixth grade on the day they showed the movie to the girls about menstruation. If she hadn't done that, I would have had perfect attendance for the whole year. She'd been remarking that none of us had ever had perfect attendance and here I was so close, and she kept me home for no reason.

These are facts! About life! That everyone knew except me. I couldn't wait for the afternoon to be over. I even considered faking sick to get home sooner. But I used the two hours to put my thoughts in order and prepared a speech that I would deliver calmly, that would reflect a mature thirteen-year-old girl, who was ready for whatever adventure life had to offer.

My mother was at the kitchen sink rinsing off a raw chicken when I burst through the screen door.

"MOM! I can't believe you haven't told me before! Everybody knows but me! It's your duty as a mother to tell me! AND. I. AM. READY."

That was the last thing I wanted to do, yell at my mother. I braced myself for a smack across the face and or a command to go to my room and a "just wait 'til your father gets home." But my mother just rested the pink crinkly carcass on the paper towels laid out on the counter, dabbed it dry and started fussing with it, touching it delicately, using only her fingertips as if she were handling fine lace or jewelry.

"What has your sister been telling you?"

"Nothing." This was true. She didn't tell me anything about "The Facts of Life."

"Did she give you another book?"

"No ..." I answered, weakly.

My mother froze a moment before shifting her focus from the chicken to me.

"You're lying. What did I tell you? There is one thing I will not tolerate –"

"A liar," I finished her sentence and handed her the now coverless, dog eared paperback from my shoulder bag. I glanced at the naked chicken carcass. It looked obscene and vulnerable, at the same time

136

alert, as if it had been listening.

I had no appetite that night and just nibbled on dry iceberg lettuce and raw carrots as I watched the others rip into the legs, thighs, and breasts that my mother had "shaked 'n baked." She had assured me that she would say nothing to either Patty or my father until she had read the book.

After my mother completed her evening ablutions of showering and massaging an assortment of creams and lotions into every inch of skin and brushing her hair one hundred strokes, she put on her white satin night gown and robe ensemble with matching silk slippers, and sat down on the couch with Rosemary's Baby. She looked beautiful and saintly, like Mary in 'The Pieta', holding a paperback instead of the body of Christ. I watched her read from the staircase, ready to dart upstairs on all fours whenever she took a bathroom or cigarette break, but she never did. She continued through the entire book.

After she turned the last page and closed the cover, she took in a slow deep breath, exhaled, and called, "Cassie? I know you're there. I know you're on the staircase."

"No I'm not!" I blurted.

"Come here please." I scooted off the staircase and shuffled across the floor to the sofa.

"Am I in trouble? Patty gave me the book!"

"The next time your sister gives you something to read, show it to me first. Promise?"

Again, with the promises! Did they really think it did any good?

"I promise." At that moment I really meant it. My mother sat silently, staring me down into an uncomfortable silence which I broke with, "Patty said it was scary. I didn't think it was scary at all."

She lowered her eyes and replied, "I didn't think it was scary either."

Wow. We're agreeing. Maybe I could ask her – no. I better not. "So, Mom, what does 'lodging his hardness' mean?" My voice was a shrill.

My mother turned her full body towards me and pointed her right index finger like a gun.

"First of all, don't ever say those filthy words again!"

"But why are they filthy? That's what I don't understand!"

She clasped her hands onto her clenched lap and continued, "Because what happens between a man and a woman is a very beautiful and sacred thing and it shouldn't be talked about in that way. When a man and woman get married, they will want to have children."

She looked up at the blank television screen across the room, for reassurance and maybe instructions. "So in order to have children, they must 'make love.'" This was beginning to sound religious.

"Which means, at night, in the bed, they kiss and hug and then the man puts his penis inside the woman... down there – and..." Creepy religious.

My mother was doing a good job of pretending not to be uncomfortable, but I knew she was. I knew she hated having to talk to me about the human body, alone and serious. Usually, she was quipping witty out the side of her mouth. When my little brother asked her where babies came from, she told him: "The freezer bin with the chickens and roast beefs."

But she soldiered on "... and then the sperm comes out of the man's penis and fertilizes the woman's eggs – and it is all very beautiful and sacred – and that's how the baby is made. Then the woman carries the baby while it grows inside her stomach for nine months and then the baby comes out – down there." She took a breath and exhaled, then looked at my dumbfounded face. It was clearly my turn to talk.

"And this is okay with God?"

"Why yes, of course. God made our bodies – the woman's and the man's this way so we could have children."

Why was I the last person on earth to know this?

"Oh. So you and Dad did this four times?" She opened her mouth to speak, closed it, and then reopened.

"Well, we... Yes. Yes, we did."

A picture of my father flicked on in my brain. His face was handsome, but I couldn't see any end to the field of black hair that covered his arms, legs, and chest. "Was it horrible?" I asked.

"Of course not!" She said that like it was a well-known fact.

"So what does 'lodging his hardness' mean?" Why wouldn't she give me a straight answer?

"What did I just tell you? I told you never to say those words again. Those words are a dirty way of describing the way a man's penis must get to be able to plant the seed inside the woman."

"Hard?"

"Well, yes..."

"I am NEVER EVER going to do that!" I screamed. My mother countered with an almost as loud voice.

"That's exactly what I said when I was your age!" She was looking at me with camaraderie. A look I'd never seen. She had seemed to be aging through this discussion, and now suddenly she looked like she could be my sister, and she wanted to jump back in time into my world and venture down that primrose path with me.

"Really?" I said with too much enthusiasm.

My mother's face rewound itself back to seriousness and motherhood.

"But when you're married and you're in love, you'll feel differently." Somehow, I did not fully believe her.

"NO. I. WON'T.

"YES. YOU. WILL."

"NO! I won't." I could keep this up all night.

"Yes you – okay, it's time for you to get to bed. Is there anything else you want to ask me?"

"Yea. What's an orgasm?" My mother swallowed hard, took a deep breath, and stood up on her exhale.

"I don't know."

Boogers

Sister Rose Virginia wore her habit like moisturizer. It was absolutely form-fitting, accentuating her hourglass figure with its big boobs. She loved strutting her holy package around, shaking her rosary like a maraca. She especially loved strutting it all in front of Mr. McCullen, the janitor. She'd deliberately knock a thermostat knob off the wall, a window shade down or a door off its hinges, anything to get him into her classroom. Once the poor guy was there, she'd stretch her vertebrae up to its full five-foot-four, nudge her habit off her face releasing a sprig of copper hair, and shove her bib to one side where one full, round, firm C cup was begging to be noticed under that thick sheath of black nylon. She was a woman underneath all those black robes, and she had urges. That was certainly obvious to us, the thirty-eight eighth grade girls under her tutelage at Our Lady of Perpetual Sorrow grade school in Cloverdale, Pennsylvania.

Sister Rose seemed to mock my everlasting pre-pubescent status. If there were such a section in the Guinness Book of World Records, you'd find my name as the last female of her generation to start her period. In another related chapter, I'd be listed as the youngest female ever to

141

apply a razor to her legs. My mother made me. That was the one area I was blooming in – hair. Having an excess of hair without starting my period or developing breasts seemed abnormal. I started to worry that I might be a lesbian. I wasn't entirely sure what a lesbian was, but I'd heard it had something to do with not being completely female and it looked like that was the direction I was heading for with my flat chest, disproportionally long hairy legs, big feet, and strong nose.

All the other eighth-grade girls were growing more beautiful by the day. Their hair was silkier and shiner and growing in one direction. Their freckles were fading into tans, accentuating their bright white straight smiles and – they all wore bras. I was still wearing an undershirt yet had to buy my shoes in the women's department.

When Sister Rose wasn't flaunting her repressed sexuality in front of Mr. McCullen, she'd pick her nose. She'd give us huge writing assignments, forcing our focus downwards, while she'd sit at her desk and dig away with glee. She could have had a 'G' spot up one of those crannies. It was a real challenge, to catch her picking, without her catching you catch her. If she did catch you catch her, you were in for a fall. You'd think she'd be ashamed of herself — but no, Sister Rose was an angry, frustrated young woman responsible for the education and welfare of thirty-eight thirteen-year-old girls, seven hours a day. When caught with a finger up her nostril, she was not going to concede – she was going to attack. God help you. She'd squint up her tiny olive eyes, tighten her dry, thin-lipped mouth and give you a look that said: "Just...you...wait..."

I was really good at catching her. By the middle of the school year, she was almost as good at catching me catch her, but not quite. The game had become very interesting. By June we were knocking heads. One day she caught me and gave me a look that haunted me for many years. Her freckles turned a Jack O' Lantern orange and her breasts seemed to engorge, causing her bib to rise up almost parallel to her desk. She didn't even take her finger out of her nose. She kept staring right at me with a weird smile on her face. I immediately dropped my head and went back to the pointless assignment of writing our favorite memories of Our Lady of Perpetual Sorrow, which I had finished with one sentence. Every ounce of blood in my body had rushed to my face and my heart was pounding so hard, my body was vibrating. Embarrassment for Boogers, (her nickname) had somehow become an embarrassment for me.

Later that week she summoned Mr. McCullen into the classroom to fix a clothes bar in the cloak closet, which she had knocked down. It was June. No one was wearing a cloak. Mr. McCullen arrived, toolbox in hand. Boogers arched her back, lifted her chest, thrust her habit back and strutted across the front of the room with outstretched arms as if she were welcoming him onto a cruise ship, or into a brothel.

"Mr. McCullen, I don't know how it happened! It just... fell down!"

The fallen clothes bar lay motionless at their feet. We could almost believe that it had unhitched itself from the wall, and taken a nosedive onto the classroom floor, in an attempt to escape the boredom of a desolate cloak closet.

Mr. McCullen gave it a little tap with his boot as he removed the toothpick from his teeth. "It's a clothes bar, Sister."

"Why, yes, it is Mr. McCullen!" She replied with the gusto of a game show contestant.

Mr. McCullen held his toothpick between his finger tips like a cigar, which I knew he smoked before Christmas and summer vacations. It was as if his fingers were rehearsing and really craving that moment when they'd be holding the real thing which was just days away. "There are much more urgent matters to attend to, Sister! Didja know there was a urinal overflowin' on da first floor?"

"No! I did not know that!" Boogers said as she curled a short thin strand of orangey hair with her fingers. Both parties' hands were wishing they were holding or doing something else.

Mr. McCullen continued, pointing with the toothpick for emphasis. "So, consequently, all the water fountains are sprouting hot water!"

"Really?" Boogers' body was twisted in all four directions – upper body east; hips and stomach south; thighs west; calves north. The air in the room began to feel dirty and thick with sin. I didn't know who to feel more mortified for. Mr. McCullen may have heard my thoughts as he kept his eyes above her nose where her brain might be.

He shouted, "It's eighty-two degrees! Do you want the children to dehydrate?" As he marched towards the door fuming, we caught each other's eye. He relaxed for a moment, nodded his head and called to me, "How ya doin', Missy Cassie?" and without waiting for an answer, he exited the room.

Mr. McCullen was my parents go to person for all things plumbing and had become a friend to our family. Sister Rose did not know this. As much as this acknowledgement warmed my heart, I almost wished he hadn't done that. Boogers and I caught each other's eye. War was declared. She would get me back big time.

That afternoon Boogers decided to distribute our school portraits, which had been taken in January and sitting on her desk for two weeks. She was giving each one a silent critique with her animated Irish face before placing an identity onto them.

"Kathleen Donato? I almost didn't recognize you under all those eyebrows, Kathleen." We held our breath as Kathleen slumped back to her desk in shame with her free hand covering her forehead, her portrait clutched against her chest as Boogers continued her emotional execution with glee.

"Linda Warner?"

Linda responded as if to an actual question. "Yes, Sister?" Boogers held up her picture in lieu of saying outright – "Your picture, stupid!"

"Oh! Yeah!" Linda giggled and lumbered on up to the front of the room with her perpetual smile on her face, which even Boogers' nasty commentary could not erase.

"Braces, Linda, braces. Or stop smiling. The choice is yours." Linda made her way back to her desk, displaying her picture with pride, as Boogers went on to her next victim.

"Maureen Crosby?" Boogers held her hand to her chest, like she was having heartburn, as she handed Maureen her picture. "Maureen, Maureen, tsk, tsk, tsk. Well, you've got brains. You can thank the Lord for that." Maureen rolled her eyes and mouthed something like 'asshole' or the equivalent of 'mother-fucker' to the class. We all laughed into our hands.

I was trying to act cool and calm, while on the inside I was panicking, expecting the worst of pictures and feedback from this monster woman who was now smiling with joy at one photo.

"Angela Andreoli!" Angela had grown into herself and gone from a skinny metallic screechy girl into a tall voluptuous brunette with a straight white smile, in a matter of weeks. It was unsettling.

"Congratulations Angela!" Boogers was confusing good looks with good grades! I was pretending to write while I was watching Boogers as she picked up one portrait, stared at it a moment and smiled to herself. It was a scary smile that exposed her yellow eyeteeth and bugged out her pea-green eyes. She then set it aside on her desk, next to a box of tissues. She continued to hand out the photos until the pile was depleted, except for that one lone picture next to the tissues, which I knew was mine. I was sure of it as soon as I saw those yellow eyeteeth emerge.

The fact was I never took a good picture because I refused to smile. I didn't realize it then, but I was on my way to becoming an existentialist. What did I care about a stupid picture? It was what was inside a person that was important. Wasn't that part of the Catholic doctrine? Wasn't vanity a sin?

I was giving 'ol Boogers a game face as I walked up to her desk. I wasn't going to wait for her to call on me. I was taking the initiative, attacking first. She was filing her nails with a butter knife.

"Is that my picture?"

"I'm not sure who this person is." She snipped back.

"Well, it's probably me, since I'm the only one who didn't get their picture back." She stopped filing and slipped the knife under the desk blotter.

"You tell me." Boogers held up the picture like a dirty diaper. "Is this sour looking girl, you?" Sour? I hated how adults used that word in the sixties and seventies to describe unhappy children.

It was not a good picture. The guy must have had a magnifying glass on his lens. There were things on my face not visible to the human eye. To make matters worse, my mother had insisted on setting my hair the night before with Dippity-Do and Spoolies. It looked like I had a spare tire incubating on my head. But all that was going through my head at that very moment was: Is this how the world sees me? My mother's friends told me I looked like Elizabeth Taylor in National Velvet. They were probably pumped up on coffee and having a hot flash when they said that, but still, this picture could not be me!

Tears were running down my face. Boogers was silently chuckling to herself. What was God thinking about all this? He couldn't be too happy with this kind of behavior in one of his brides of Christ. I could hear whispers and giggles coming from the class. Whose side were they on?

"Your nose is running." Boogers was holding out a tissue to me. I took it and began to wipe up the fluids trickling from my face. One tissue was obviously not enough. Boogers saw this and violently yanked another out of the box. I continued to dry my eyes and blow my nose. My face was still damp, but this time I had to appeal to her for another.

"Still not finished? Would you like another?"

"Yes, please." I was about to break into sobs.

She slowly, with a tease, drew the tissue from the box, as if she were pulling a sheet off a lover, gently waking him. The scenario had now become about tissues.

"Tsk, tsk, tsk, such a messy girl."

Okay, that was way below the belt to be legal. Game over! I was going for the kill. "Sister Rose, if you have this big box of Kleenexes on your desk, why don't you use them instead of your fingers?"

A sheath of ice encompassed the room. Everything froze. Time. Space. Dust bunnies. She looked like she was going to implode. There was nothing else she could do to me. Vatican II was in session. Corporal punishment was no longer an acceptable outlet for sexual frustration among the celibate clergy.

Mr. McCullen rapped on the door and entered at the same time, practically taking the door with him as he walked over to the desk and picked up my picture.

"Why, you got the map of Ireland on your face. A lovely Colleen you are Missy Cassie with your beautiful green eyes!"

My eyes? I hadn't even looked at my eyes in the picture. But Mr. McCullen had. This man had radar. He was my superhero. I wanted a Monkee's song to play now. I wanted to be lifted up by several handsome men like Mickey Dolenz and Mr. McCullen and carried along the sands of California!

"Mr. McCullen?" Boogers called.

Damn! Boogers' nasty, higher than usual pitched voice brought me back to Our Lady of Perpetual Sorrow and the East Coast.

"Mr. McCullen?!" Boogers, now in the role of jilted lover, her well of flirtations run dry, with nothing left to fix or break, asked, "Why are you here?" Not only jilted lover – a superior being, grasping to maintain an ounce of dignity.

"Oh. Didn't I leave me toolbox here?" Mr. McCullen answered.

"No, you did not." Boogers responded steely, through her clenched jaw.

"Oh well then, I'll be off. As soon as I see Missy Cassie here give us a smile. Ya been cryin' I see. Maybe ya need a cold drink. The blasted fountains aren't workin' properly, so why don't I take ye down to the cafeteria and get ye some orange juice?"

We were out the door before Boogers could object. The grades were in. We were just biding time in that stuffy classroom, heeding the state's regulations. Although I was grateful for Mr. McCullen's interception, I'm still curious as to what Boogers would have done. I think Mr. McCullen's rescue was meant more for her than for me. I think he was saving her from herself.

Mrs. Evans

Shelly Evans was my closest friend from kindergarten through eighth grade. We lived on an oval shaped block of twin homes in Cloverdale, a suburb outside Philadelphia. Shelly's backyard was slightly diagonal from mine, separated by a white ranch-style fence. She had three scary brothers who I couldn't tell apart unless they stood up or spoke. Two were older, one was younger – each held their own private rage at the universe with pride.

Her brothers were attractive with nicely shaped heads and thick brown hair, lean bodies, brown eyes, celestial noses and wide mouths flanked with a dimple or two. Not that they'd take an inkling of an inventory of me. I was their sister's friend and it was their duty to hate their sister if they wanted any respect from each other or the other boys on the block.

It was never clear to me what Mr. Evans's job actually was other than it involved travelling, custom fit suits, frequent haircuts, and polished shoes. It was known, however, that he was an only child from a Jewish family in North Philadelphia, but had converted to Catholicism shortly after meeting Shelly's mom.

There were also at any given time an indeterminable number of cats dwelling in and around their house. No sisters. Just a mom who looked like she could be Shelly's older sister.

The first time I ever saw Mrs. Evans, she was ringing up groceries at the A&P.

From where I was, two aisles over and four years old, she looked and sounded like a movie star princess. I didn't have much contact with anyone outside my immediate family. My weekdays were spent watching and helping my mother feed, clothe, and bathe my baby brother Freddy. On Saturdays my two older siblings and father slept in late and would then appear at the kitchen table rumpled and bleary-eyed hovering over bowls of cereal and cups of instant coffee.

Once my father had a sufficient amount of coffee in him and responded to my mother with coherent sentences, she and I would take off in the station wagon to do the week's grocery shopping. I loved going to the A&P and riding in the baby seat, until I no longer fit, then inside the cart with the groceries. It felt like I was in an amusement park. When the butchers popped out of the mirrored walls behind the meat cases and tossed packages of meat into the bins, I'd scream with delight and horror. I thought I'd won the jackpot when I found open boxes of Oreos or Ginger Snaps spilling onto the shelves. I'd grab a handful when my mom was busy reading the ingredients on a box or gabbing with another mother.

I just didn't like 'check out time' because my mother would always go to Mrs. Krieghoffer's aisle. Mrs. Krieghoffer looked like a big Chatty Baby Doll. She had a chunky pink body and face with bright-yellow hair and a wart that looked like Captain Kangaroo's head on the cleft in her chin. Her butt was so huge it locked her into place in front of the register. There was no evidence or ever a mention of Mrs. Krieghoffer's life outside of the A&P. She could have been born in the checkout aisle or maybe the A&P was built around her.

She and my mom were kindred spirits, both sharing a high standard of shopping ethics. She appreciated the way my mother unloaded her grocery cart, sorting the sundries from the food, the frozen from the fresh, the packaged from the dairy, and so on. In return, Mrs. Krieghoffer would give my mother extra trading stamps which my mom used to upgrade our kitchen with more modern appliances, such as a blender and electric can opener.

Mrs. Krieghoffer took her job and money very seriously and did not allow talking at her register. The other cashiers knew better than to ask for change or a price check when Mrs. Krieghoffer was in the midst of a ring up. The one time the store manager came over to ask her about a schedule change, she pushed all the groceries back onto the ramp and started ringing up all over again.

My mother's trust and confidence in Mrs. Krieghoffer went so far that she would fashion her shopping plans around her schedule, which was no fun for me, especially when three aisles over there was always a noisy party going on in Mrs. Evan's aisle. Hers was the slowest moving line in the store, but her customers didn't seem to care. Mrs. Evans was laughing and chatting with them and they were laughing and chatting amongst themselves. Little kids were handed lollipops and babies were being kissed and passed around – and Mrs. Evans was conducting it all!

Even the regulation green uniform that looked like a sack of lawn sod on Mrs. Krieghoffer seemed breezy and elegant on Mrs. Evans with her caramel-colored skin and Barbie Doll shape. She dressed it up with a ruby-red necklace, matching bracelets, and earrings that jingled and sparkled when she punched the keys or picked up a frozen chicken. She wore her shiny auburn hair in a French twist, and she never seemed to stop smiling even when she was talking. Her voice and laugh were so enchanting they surpassed the din of the store noise and carried three aisles over.

I was infatuated. From my bedroom window I could see her in her yard, gardening or hanging her wash, her hair loose or in a ponytail. At church I'd see her every Sunday after the ten o'clock mass lighting candles before the Blessed Virgin, kneeling and praying. She'd wear a black chapel veil on her head like the one Jackie Kennedy wore at President Kennedy's funeral, just smaller.

The first time I saw Mr. Evans, I was helping my mother hang the sheets on the clothesline. It was about 9:30, a hot day at the end of August. In one week, I would turn six and become a first grader. I was hearing sentences like that several times a day in that last week and I'm pretty sure that was what my mother was saying to me when I stepped out of the rows of sheets we had hung to see Mr. Evans leaning on the ranch-style fence that separated our yards, looking at my mother's bare feet. His skin was the color of maple syrup and just as smooth and glossy. He was wearing a sleeveless tee shirt, denim shorts, and holding a half full bottle of Coca-Cola. He looked exotic and dangerous. He gave me a half-moon smile and a playful wink.

"Good morning, Betty!"

My mother looked out from behind the sheets, flushed and annoyed.

"Oh. Hello, Jeremy." Mr. Evans brought the bottle to his lips. "That your breakfast?" my mother asked.

"Too hot to eat." He took a long drink and emptied the bottle, too fast I thought. My mother continued fussing with the sheets, but I could tell she was watching Mr. Evans from the corners of her eyes.

"Addie working today?" she asked.

"Just dropped her off. Kids are still sleeping." He let out a belch and continued talking without excusing himself. "Last week of summer and it's a scorcher."

"Nothing much we can do about the weather." My mother picked up the laundry basket and positioned it under her arm, ready to go back into the house, but as soon as she turned her back, Mr. Evans called to her in a louder voice, "You know, Bett..?"

My mother turned only her head towards Mr. Evans who kept talking.

"You oughta get Bob to buy you a clothes' dryer. He's making enough money now."

My mother's body stiffened as she looked at him. He ran his fingers through his thick black hair, swallowed, and said in a soft almost hoarse voice, "It's a hot day. It'd be a lot easier... just throw everything in a dryer...."

She turned the rest of her body and took a step towards the fence, holding her laser stare on Mr. Evans's face. It looked like another burp was forming in his chest, but this time he kept his mouth closed tight, letting it go off inside. His cheeks puffed out and his Adam's apple swelled and glided up and down his neck as my mother waited for his face to return to normal before speaking.

"Even if I had a dryer, I'd still hang my sheets outside on a day like today rather than heat up the house with a running dryer. Do something nice for Addie and the kids – why don't you? Start by cleaning up your yard." My mother turned and started back to the house, "Let's go, Cassie."

Mr. Evans looked almost as white as my dad. Our eyes met. I felt sorry for him. I knew how hurtful my mother's words could be and I was only five! I wanted to say something to make him feel better but all I could come up with was, "The sheets smell really good when you hang them outside." I didn't wait to see the effect the words had; my courage had its limits. I turned and ran back into the house.

Shelly and I were the only girls in our class that had a birthday in September, which seemed reason enough to become friends. She looked like my Ginger Doll who was a late toddler Barbie Doll, with wider proportions. Shelly's hair was the same color and style, golden-brown falling slightly above the shoulders; her skin was a milky smooth coffee that highlighted her aqua eyes which were sometimes sparkling and other times opaque. She had a tiny brown mole below her right nostril and a crescent-moon dimple on her left cheek, which was the only thing I could see at the time that she and her mother had in common. Shelly was even more shy than me and she was willing to go along with any of my ideas.

During the month of July, the summer before sixth grade, Shelly and I were having a hopscotch marathon in the Murphy's two car driveway. The Murphy's had a corner house with a jungle gym, swing set, and above-ground pool. They also had a bungalow at the Jersey shore, where they spent the month. Their property was fair game for us not so privileged kids stuck in the hot and dusty suburbs.

Unfortunately, we couldn't get inside their house to have at their color T.V. or the jumbo state of the art refrigerator that dispensed ice cubes. So, when we felt dehydrated and sweaty, we went to my house for a time-out and cold drink. Except for Tuesdays, which was my mom's day to disinfect the house with Pine Sol and Clorox, while blasting and singing along to Herb Albert or Connie Francis. That scene was to be avoided at all costs. The probability that a waft of ammonia up our budding nasal passages along with the belting of the Tijuana Brass and roaring vacuum could cause some neurological damage was pretty high. We'd rather take a chance once a week at Shelly's house where she might get bullied and pushed around by one of her unhinged brothers.

At eleven o'clock on the second Tuesday in July, the sun had already swallowed up the entire sky. The tar was melting and bubbling in small puddles in the Murphy's driveway, and you could actually see and hear the heat as it reflected off the pavement – a high pitch electric white hum. After we had popped all the pop-able tar bubbles, we walked down the street to Shelly's house. When I stepped through the back door I went blind for a couple of seconds while my eyes adjusted to the darkness. There was a gray eerie light coming from the television in the living room, along with it, the murmuring of earnest T.V. voices and a low muffled sobbing. A look of shame crossed Shelly's face.

"I thought my mom was working today," she apologized in a whisper.

As she scurried around the kitchen looking for glasses and ice cubes, shooing cats off the counter and table, my eyes followed a trail of cigarette smoke that had drifted from the living room. There, in a tattered easy chair sat Mrs. Evans, wearing a faded terrycloth bathrobe, her hair a mousy brown mangle, drawing on a cigarette and absently stroking the ancient white Siamese asleep in her lap.

The room was so dark the T.V. cast a spotlight on her face, illuminating her pasty white tear-stained cheeks and puffy eyes. Halfway through a long exhale of smoke, she took a sip from a short glass containing a thick brown liquid and tiny melted ice cubes. After she swallowed, the remainder of smoke escaped through her nostrils. Her lips moved, but no words could be heard, just a low moan. I couldn't take my eyes off her.

Although my infatuation had ebbed through the years, I still held a special place for her. She was not making many appearances in the yard or at church as she had in the past. She was a mystery to the neighborhood and only seemed to come completely alive at the A&P.

"Here's your drink."

Shelly was holding out a glass of water to me. Our eyes met. Up until that moment I felt that I was the alpha girl in our relationship. Shelly had just become mystical and valiant to me.

"Thanks."

We drank our water in one slow gulp, avoiding eye contact, then placed the glasses in the sink and went back outside into the glaring sun to continue with our hopscotch tournament. We never spoke of that moment.

After the Christmas holiday in sixth grade, Shelly started to be absent at least once a week. I didn't see as much of her in the summer as she seemed to always have things to do at home. It was another Tuesday in August when our friendship took a step into the rabbit hole for me. My family had a tradition of going to the beach one day a year. That year, since my older siblings Patty and Greg would not be going as they were teenagers and had summer jobs, my younger brother Freddy and I could bring a friend along. I wanted to ask Linda Warner, because I was seeing more of her than Shelly and we had become closer friends.

"I want you to ask Shelly." My mother said as she handed me a plate to dry.

"Why can't I ask Linda?"

"You can ask Linda if Shelly can't go."

"But why?"

My mother sighed, turned off the water, placed her Playtex gloved hands on the sides of the sink and stared out the window. If it weren't for the small forest of maples and evergreens that now towered the houses, she would have been able to see the Evan's backyard as she could ten years prior. It looked as if she was doing just that, peering through the foliage and back in time.

"Such a shame…" she delicately shook her head then turned to me, "She's been a good friend. She won't have another chance to go to the beach this summer."

"Why?" This was tiresome, getting information piecemeal like this, making me sound like a two-year-old.

My mother turned the water back on, resumed dishwashing and groaned, "You ask too many questions."

Shelly accepted the invitation, but with a hesitancy that had been sneaking up on her for the past year. Sure enough, Michael, her middle brother, showed up in the driveway as we were pulling out. My father stomped on the brake and slammed the car into park.

"Jesus Mary and Joseph! I almost backed into you!" He shouted to the boy, who looked greasy, unkempt and oblivious as he peered through the car and my family directly to Shelly in the backseat.

"You gotta come home!"

"Why?" Shelly yelled right back at him.

"Cause Mom said!"

"She told me I could go!"

"Well, she changed her mind!"

Shelly was silent and still for a moment, her eyes seemed to be focused on something inside herself.

Michael opened the car door and yelled, "Come on already!"

Without a word or a glance at me or anyone else she gathered her beach towel under her arm, stepped out of the car, and followed her brother down the block.

"I told you I shoulda asked Linda!" I grunted to no one in particular while I wished for rain.

Shelly continued to be absent or late or come in for half days throughout the seventh and eighth grades. Sometimes we'd walk home together or hang out at lunch and recess. We'd talk and laugh about our eighth-grade teacher Sister Rose, aka Boogers, and how many times we caught her in a nose pick that day. Shelly didn't bring up anything personal and I didn't ask. She'd stopped going to the eighth-grade nine o' clock Mass on Sundays and it'd been a few years since I saw her mother lighting candles, let alone anywhere near the church.

I had stopped going shopping with my mother on a regular basis somewhere between fifth and sixth grade. When I did go, I always made a point of checking out aisle three, where four out of five times I'd see Mrs. Evans ringing up groceries. She looked a little heavier and older, but her beauty was still evident. There was no noisy party in her line. It looked like Mrs. Evans was just doing her job with efficiency, not unlike Mrs. Krieghoffer.

Shelly was absent the entire last week of eighth grade. After the final day of school, I tried calling her, but her phone had been disconnected. For the first time since that hot July morning three years earlier, I went to her house, but this time to the front door. The Evan's gold Chevy was in the driveway, so I knew somebody had to be home. The curtains were drawn on the front window and the inside door was closed, which was unusual for such a warm day. Since only a rusted stump was left of the door knocker, I used my knuckles to knock. There was no sound of movement of any kind in the house. I counted to ten and was about to knock again when I heard a fumbling and clicking sound behind the door and suddenly it sprung open the two inches the chain allowed. A waft of air that smelled like cat and heat swept across my face along with a stream of cigarette smoke.

"Who is it?" asked a disembodied voice from behind the door.

"It's Cassie, Shelly's friend."

Mrs. Evans eyes, nose, mouth and cheek bones appeared in the opening, veiled in smoke. There were a few moments of silence as her eyes studied me.

"You washed me," she slurred.

"Wha –"

"Jush a mi –," she disappeared for a second as she undid the chain and swung the door wide open. The narrow space behind Mrs. Evans was bathed in gray shadows as if the house was at war with light. A black and white striped cat sat still and tall on top of the staircase that rose above Mrs. Evan's head. She was wearing a pink plaid housecoat, and her hair was half up and half down. It looked like it had recently been a neat French twist but had since collapsed. Her face also looked like it had been made up to perfection, worn and never washed off. She pointed at me with her cigarette then brought it to her mouth.

"From the window, you used to wash – watch me."

I didn't know what to say to that. I knew exactly what she was talking about. I had no idea she ever saw me watching her. I felt at once endeared and ashamed. The striped cat was now wrapped around one of Mrs. Evans's ankles. I looked at the top of the stairs where I saw the same cat, still sitting tall. I felt a chill.

"You're a good little Catholic girl, aren't you?" She was stroking the cat with her other bare foot. Her feet were tiny and agile, her toes painted bazooka gum pink. I could feel her waiting for an answer or for me to stop looking at her legs. I picked my head up and reentered the surreal exchange.

"I guess. Where's Shelly? She wasn't at school."

Her face broke into a snarl as she barked, "WHO WANTS TO KNOW?" She lifted the cat with her foot and tossed it back into the house. "Are you a spy? Did those damn nuns send you?"

"No!"

"You tell them it's none of their beeswax where my daughter is!" Mrs. Evans took a deep draw on the cigarette then tossed it past my head onto the barren front lawn behind me.

"I can't tell them anything because today was the last day of school." The tossed cat had joined its twin on the landing. A gray feline was now on Mrs. Evans's shoulder. My eyes started tearing and my nose was running. I was allergic to cats but there also was a surplus of emotions brewing beneath my prepubescent skin. Mrs. Evans's face collapsed.

"Hey, what's the matter? Why you crying? You think I hurt her, my own kid? I love her! I just needed her with me. That no good father –" With that last statement she slid down the wall and collapsed onto the floor. The cat held its balance on her shoulder.

Shelly appeared on the staircase between the two striped felines that seemed to have grown and been cast in bronze, like pillars.

"Come on inside, Mom." Her voice was deep and hoarse.

"That you baby? You get your sleep?" Mrs. Evans was rustling in her housecoat pockets and pulled out a cigarette and lighter.

"What are you doing here, Cassie?" Shelly was now in shadow on the staircase, which made her sound even more cold and distant. If asked, I would not be able to tell where the pain I was feeling at that moment was located; if it was sharp or dull, but only that it was a ten on the scale and the worst I'd ever felt.

"Your lildle frrend here was worried about you." A clowder of cats had gathered on and around Mrs. Evans's legs and lap, the gray one still atop her shoulder. She was attempting to flick her ashes out the door, which was still open as I had not moved and was still holding the screen door open with my back.

"She doesn't know what a shit you have for a father!"

160

"Mom! Get! Up!" Shelly screamed as if she were begging for her life. This family was well into the rabbit hole, and I was witnessing and perhaps even causing them to sink deeper. Coming here was clearly a mistake.

"Don't talk to me like that," Mrs. Evans growled back, "like I'm a piece of dirt. Like your father talks to me!" The growls transcended into sobs. Her cigarette slipped from her fingers. Shelly came running down the stairs, knelt by her mother, and wrapped an arm around her.

"Shhh, Mom? Mommy? It's okay. Come on inside. It's almost time for your shows." She had coaxed her mother to her feet and was trying to pull her out of the doorway. The two striped cats were watching from the landing. The others were tossing the lit cigarette around like a hockey puck. Shelly looked at me without making eye contact.

"You should go home, Cassie." I opened my mouth to say something but nothing came out. Mrs. Evans was bent over trying to pick up her cigarette. Shelly kicked it out the door with her bare foot. "Come on, Mom." They turned and headed back into the house. Over her shoulder Shelly's last words were, "Go home, Cassie," as she slammed the inside door shut with her foot.

Somehow Shelly was able to graduate from Our Lady of Perpetual Sorrow. She attended the graduation as did Mrs. Evans and the three brothers. There was a party for the graduates and their families in the cafeteria after the ceremony. Basically, it was paper cups of Kool Aid and cupcakes, courtesy of the Sodality. Afterwards, we all went our separate ways, eager to get home and out of our uniforms for the last time.

I didn't see Shelly at all that summer. She and I went to different high schools. The Evans's were the first family in the parish to get a divorce. They were no longer welcome at church and the youngest brother, Danny, had to finish his last three years at the public school.

I thought of the times I saw Mrs. Evans in church, kneeling before the Blessed Virgin after Mass in her black chapel veil. I wondered what she was praying for and if God ever heard her prayers, and if so, why didn't he listen to them?

High Drama

Saint Bernadette's Academy, a girls' private high school in Willow Park, Pennsylvania, was a mix of upper-middle class beauties who were star athletes and/or scholars; lower-middle class scholarship girls; and younger sisters of alumnae or upper classmen. My sister Patty was a senior when I entered as a freshman. She was in the scholarship group, and somewhat athletic and exuded extraordinary confidence.

Although my three siblings went to the same Catholic grade school as I did, their education was far better than mine. Out of the eleven teachers I had in eight years, only three of them had a positive influence on me. The other eight frightened, bored, or confused me. It was as if I was in a completely different school on a parallel universe. The truth was, I did not do well on the entrance exam to St. Bernadette's and should not have been accepted. However, my mother thought that I would be put in 'basket weaving' if I were to go to the public school where everyone was accepted. She made a case for me with the board of the academy, appealed to their Christian duty, and persuaded them to accept me. (My mother and Patty told me about this many years later).

Most people, including faculty, students, even maintenance, were surprised to learn that Patty and I were related.

"You're Patty's sister? No way!" seemed to be the refrain through the halls and classrooms of Saint Bernadette's those first few agonizing days. It needed to stop or change to something like, "Oh. That makes sense," or even just, "Oh." No opinion, just recognition of the fact. But even that would require an accomplishment.

I needed to 'make' something, which meant I had to display talent and competence in a sport or club, be judged, and then accepted. Activities open to freshmen were: hockey, cheerleading, newspaper, debate club, and sodality. I signed up for everything and immediately made sodality without even trying out, which I thought indicated a lack of discernment on their part, or a loving generosity. I had no idea what 'sodality' was, but rather than ask someone and look like an idiot for signing up for something I knew nothing about, I decided to just show up for the meeting which was at lunch time that very same day.

As I was climbing the last lap of stairs to the third floor, Patty and a gang of seniors were coming down. She stopped me on the landing.

"Third floor is for seniors only."

"I have a meeting." As I tried to walk around her, she blocked me with her body.

"You have a meeting? You've been here two days!"

"So?" I took a step to her other side, but her reflexes were quicker than mine and she blocked me again.

"That's hysterical."

"Let me go!"

"What kind of meeting?" At that moment several girls, a nun, and two adult women, passed us as they made their way to the third floor. They nodded and smiled in a solemn fashion before stepping onto the last flight of stairs. It was a slow-moving group as a few of the girls were chubby and one looked like she had some kind of paralysis I'd never seen before. Once they cleared the last step Patty turned to me and cried, "Sodality? That's your meeting?" She was doubled over, mouth wide open, laughing in silence.

"What's so funny?"

She sobered up too quickly and said, "Nothing. Nothing's funny. You'll love sodality," then took off down the stairs laughing in full volume.

Room 312 was the first classroom on the right. I stood at the back door taking a read of the room. At first glance it looked full, but with a more focused eye I saw it was a scattering of about eight heavy girls, a few teachers, two nuns, and a priest. There was also the girl with paralysis sitting next to an unusually tiny girl who was evenly proportioned but of the height and build of an average six-year-old. Most of the girls had covered their desktops with opened napkins, like tablecloths, and were eating sandwiches and taking sips of milk through paper straws from cartons. The room seemed hazy and several degrees warmer than the hallway with its cool marble floors and walls.

The priest was part sitting, mostly leaning, casually on the edge of the teacher's desk, smiling as he spoke in a low but not confidential volume to one of the nuns who was sitting in a front row seat. There seemed to be a few soft conversations happening throughout the room. According to the clock on the wall, the meeting would have started ten minutes ago, but the atmosphere in the room was relaxed and informal. My stomach started growling, loudly. I stepped away from the doorway. I wasn't ready to be pulled into the milk toasty room. Was this the meeting? Or, were they in hold, possibly waiting for me? Suddenly the room went silent, followed by a chorus of voices: "In the name of the Father and of the Son and the Holy Ghost." I ran down the hall in the other direction, not sure where I was heading, but certain that sodality was not the antidote for attaining star status.

That left the debate club, newspaper, hockey, and cheerleading. Since I didn't feel smart enough to argue or write about things I didn't know or care about, that left hockey or cheerleading, and Miss Reinagel controlled both.

Miss Reinagel had a face like Napoleon Solo and the hair style of Illya Kuryakin – the dreamboat duo from The Man From Uncle – and the cunning of both, a combination that worked in her favor as coach and gym teacher for a reputable Catholic girls' academy. For Miss Reinagel, assembling the fall line-up of hockey players and cheerleaders was comparable to marshalling a platoon for the Tet Offensive. She lacked the skills and patience to contend with sensitive girls who needed that second chance. Freshmen were no exception.

My competition were strong, confident debutants from the southern tip of the Main Line. They were all-round athletes seasoned with ballet lessons and seaside summers – swimming, surfing, and soaking up the good life. The first time I picked up a hockey stick was three days before the tryouts. I had yet to grow into my size nine feet and with my long skinny legs tripped over my own stick while running within the first thirty seconds on the field and skinned both knees and my right elbow. Apparently, I was a bleeder and that was grounds for disqualification – "for my own good."

After that debacle and humiliation, there was no way I could muster the courage to try out for cheerleading. The thought of slamming a hockey ball across an open field was cathartic, while jumping around gracefully, smiling, and calling out positive reinforcements to a group that rejected me could not possibly come naturally.

The second week of my freshman year I resumed my after-school ritual of watching The Three Stooges with my eleven-year-old brother,

Freddy. I didn't really like the Stooges. Their black and white violent world left me feeling hopeless and nauseated. After one week at Saint Bernadette's, my little brother's vivacious flatulence just wasn't funny anymore. It was god damn depressing when I pictured those beautiful upper-class girls with their silky pony tails and smooth brown legs gliding down the hockey field into the sinking September sun, while I watched Mo bang Curly's and Larry's heads together. Something had to change. I needed to think.

Patty was up against the mirror, tugging at her eyebrows with a shiny hostile instrument. Our eyes met in the glass.

"What?" She barked.

"None of your business!" I belly flopped onto my twin bed. Just eleven more months and Patty would be at nursing school and the room would be completely mine! I could clean it up and think in peace. My sister refused to accept the fact that what looked like sitting and staring into space was actually thinking. According to Patty, if one had nothing else to do, one could always be improving one's looks. I knew deep down she was right, but I wouldn't even know where to begin. My face was doing things on its own. I avoided mirrors as much as possible.

"What happened? You get kicked out of Sodality?" She snorted, then opened her mouth wide and stomped her foot, laughing soundlessly. She was her favorite fan.

"It's not funny!" I threw my Lamb Chop puppet at her. She caught it with one hand and threw it back at me – hard. I ducked my head and it slammed into the wall and ricocheted into my lap.

"I hate you!" I cried. She didn't care who she hurt or how much. Why couldn't I have a nice big sister like some of the other girls at Saint Bernadette's – who ate lunch with them and braided their hair? Patty was at the foot of my bed. Was she going to sit down? Did I want her to?

"You know, instead of moping around here like you are so tortured and everything, I have a great idea!" She dropped knees first onto the bottom of my bed.

"What?" Join the convent? The Salvation Army? The circus? From now on I would never ever trust a word she said. Was she going to sit down or get up?

She started bouncing in place, "You should join the drama club! I mean, you are a born actress."

An actress?! This was something to sit up for. That idea had never crossed my mind. Didn't you have to be pretty or rich to be an actress?

"What drama club? There wasn't any sign-up sheet for that."

"That's because they're really picky and they don't want a bunch of untalented freshmen signing up 'cause they can only take one or two people.'"

"Why aren't you in the drama club?" She bounced herself off the bed and back to the mirror.

"They asked me, but I am soooo busy."

"With what?"

"Stuff." She was picking at her face with the tweezers.

"What stuff? You're not on any team or club –"

"What do you know? I'm everywhere in that school helping out! And with Mom working, who do you think makes dinner every night and cleans?"

"We all do!"

"Listen, do you want me to help you become an actress or not? I don't hafta, you know."

"Yeah, okay. You really think –?"

"Definitely! With that big forehead."

"Huh?" Was this going to get mean? "It suits my face! Mom said."

"And you are so emotional – all good for acting."

168

Patty dramatically grabbed her stomach and hunched over. Who was the better actress here?

"God this is the worst period! You are so lucky yours hasn't started yet. Maybe you'll never get one! Wouldn't that be great?!"

WHAT?! Was that even possible? Could that be what was happening to me???

"NO! It wouldn't!" I screamed. Patty's spine straightened itself out.

"See what I am talking about?" She snapped her fingers with both hands and pointed at me. "Born. Actress."

She picked up her tweezers and went back to the mirror assessing the right brow while I tried to regain a normal breathing pattern.

"The only thing is…" She continued tugging and yanking at her face, "you have to do an audition to get into the drama club."

Oh no! Not more try-outs, rejection, humiliation. Wasn't there something in life that was fun and meaningful with no chance of getting your feelings hurt?

"What's an audition?" I asked, resigned.

"It's like a speech, but with emotion and a situation."

"Where am I going to find one of those?"

"Do I look like a library? Ask Greg, he was in a play once. Remember? Last year?"

It was true. We had all piled into the car on a Saturday night to see our older brother in his theatrical debut. He didn't come onstage 'til the last scene.

"Yeah, I remember."

"He's in his room."

"The door's closed."

"So? He's not doing anything important. Knock on it."

After three knocks my brother opened his door with too much

bravado, I thought.

"Well hey there!" Sometimes I wondered if he knew who I was.

"You changed your hair."

"No, I didn't." His room smelled like old books.

"Okay, then! So." We didn't know how to talk to each other.

"I hafta do an audition to get into the drama club so Patty said to ask you because you were in that play –"

"The Death and Life of Sneaky Fitch!" He displayed the title with his entire upper body, framing large placards for each word with his long arms. "I still remember my line!" He took a mannequin like pose, "'Doc?'" My brother waited for more information to come to him from somewhere inside his head and when it didn't, he relaxed back into himself and made eye contact with me.

"That was it? That's all you said?"

He appealed to the stuffed pheasant on his dresser for clues. The bird held its one eye stare. After about ten seconds, he returned to our conversation.

"I didn't do an audition! You gotta do an audition to get a good part. You should do Antigone!"

"What's Antigone?" It sounded painful.

"A Greek Tragedy by Sophocles, she's buried alive for burying her brother! I gotta copy." He dove under his bed and quickly returned triumphant with a thin, tattered, paper-back, which he shoved into my hands.

"Here. Do the part where she's talking to Creon!"

"Crayon?"

"CREEON! I can't explain anymore. Go on, get outta here and start reading. I gotta figure out what to bring back to my dorm room."

The pheasant caught my eye on my way out, which reaffirmed a theory Freddy and I shared – the pheasant was only sometimes dead. I hoped Greg would decide to take it with him. But they probably didn't allow pets – alive, dead, or in between – in the dorm. He was a first year psychology major – on scholarship.

I read the entire script that very night. I was born to play Antigone. She was angry and so was I! But Antigone was willing to die for her convictions. I had a hard time facing a weekend alone in my room, grounded. I hoped that by playing her, some of her courage would rub off on me. Patty helped me prepare for the audition. I wore one of her silky full slips and sprinkled dry leaves in my hair. We figured she was out in the woods, so she'd be sure to have some evidence of that. I covered my face with a pale pancake base, lined my eyes with thick black liner, and painted my lips a Frosty Blue.

"You are gorgeous!" My sister was beaming with pride. I looked in the mirror. Well, I didn't look like me, that was for sure.

"Patty, do you really think her lips would be blue?"

"You are about to be buried! In the ground! Alive! All pigment has drained from your face. Remember: You. Are. Tortured!" My sister had never paid so much attention to me. I couldn't let her down.

I walked out onto the stage in Saint Bernadette's gym into the fluorescent lights. All eyes and ears were on me. Sister Elizabeth – the Principal, Miss Findlay – the English teacher, Antoinette Mascola – the drama club president, and the other senior members. But I was not me. I was a brave girl living in another country, in another century, appealing to the gods for justice!

"Then why not do it now?" I cried to the clock on the back wall. "No chance of reconciliation. I can't think of a finer reason for dying – Guilty of having buried my brother!" I raised my right fist in defiance as Patty had instructed me to do.

The list went up at 11:15 the next morning. I was the only freshman who made the club. The one other freshman who auditioned was an overachiever who tried out for everything. She had already made the hockey team, the school newspaper, and debate club. It wasn't physically possible for her to partake in all the activities. Some team captain or club president was going to get a "thanks, but no thanks." The drama club was a non-conformist group of scholarship girls, whose members let all their hair dry, color, and grow naturally, and carried tethered copies of Thus Spake Zarathustra and The Feminine Mystique in their Macramé shoulder bags. They were not about to open themselves up for a rejection from a snotty debutante, Patty said.

Antoinette Mascola, the President of the club, came from a family with 'Mob' ties – vaguely, but still. Her father was the president of the Knights of Columbus as was his father before him and so on and so on. Although she considered herself an intellectual card-carrying-socialist, her dad dressed and smelled better than she did and had her back, Patty said.

Miss Findlay, the English teacher who usually directed the main productions, opted out that year as the seniors were eager to bring in one of their own, a fellow socialist – Ian Stahl, a Philosophy grad student at Swarthmore College and editor of a "groundbreaking" newspaper Marxmen. Ian had long hair, a long nose, and long fingers. He dressed in faded black pants with maroon madras shirts and had a clubfoot.

"He is so gorgeous! And tortured!" Patty was prancing around our bedroom in her powder blue C cup bra and matching panties. Could we have different fathers?

"I wonder if he needs a stage manager. I could do that!"

My mother had sent me upstairs to hurry her up or we were going to miss the 7:25 train. I was sitting on the edge of my bed, fighting the urge to lie back down. Patty slept to the last possible minute and was ready and out the door in fifteen minutes looking 'fresh as a daisy' as

Barry the train conductor would tell her every morning. She was behind schedule today, wasting time admiring herself in her new underwear after a surgical removal of the price and size tags with nail scissors.

She'd finally gotten her white blouse buttoned. I was sure the blue and lace would be visible through the blouse, but it wasn't. Patty could get away with anything.

"Where's the club meeting today?"

"Why do you want to –?"

"'Cause, I'm coming to your meeting." Patty was out of the room and down the stairs before I was on my feet. What just happened? My mother was screaming up the stairs, "Catherine! If you're not down here in two seconds you're going to miss the train!"

We made the 7:25, barely. Barry was holding the door as we came running down the hill to the platform.

The first official drama club meeting was in the classroom where the sodality meeting was held. Sister Mary Martin, a petite redhead who looked exactly like the actress, Mary Martin, who played Peter Pan, was the overseer of extra-curricular activities and opened her classroom to any club that needed a place to meet. Patty was sitting at Ian's side on the edge of Mary Martin's desk. Mary Martin was sitting in a student's desk in the front row talking to them. Patty was holding a stack of white papers and a clip board. There was a pen behind her ear. The first two rows of seats were taken up with other members and their books and bags. I didn't feel it my place to inconvenience an upper-classman into stopping their conversation and moving their stuff to the floor or elsewhere. I started a new row and took the end seat by the window.

Patty was looking directly at me with a haughty face. "You made it."

"I'm not late."

"Nobody said you were."

Sister Mary Martin stood up, smiling, looking more like Peter Pan than Mary Martin.

"Cathy, come sit here. I'll be leaving. I just want to say a few words before I do."

Great. Now all the attention was on me as she watched and waited as I fumbled my way through the tangle of desks and bags.

"It's Cassie, Sister," Patty said.

"Cassie? How extraordinary!" Mary Martin seemed to be levitating.

Now Patty had the whole room's attention. "I gave the name to her when I was three. Every time I tried to say "CaTHy – CaSSie came out."

Ian was smiling at her. "Cute," he said.

Patty smiled back, "I was three. I couldn't control my tongue I guess." Patty shrugged and looked over at Mary Martin who was still smiling but her feet were back on the ground as she addressed the room.

"Lovely. Lovely story. Well, I just want to welcome everyone. This is the first time I've had a group of thespians in my classroom and I find that very exciting!" Mary Martin started going on and on about her thespian life being cut short when she entered the convent until Ian interrupted and said he had a 'gig in Philly' later and had to catch a train. We needed to get on with auditions.

"Of course you do. Just make sure you close the windows and put the desks back in order. How very exciting." Mary Martin flittered out of the room. More Tinkerbell than Peter, I thought. Wait a minute, did he say "auditions?"

"Thank you, Sister!" Patty called over her shoulder as she handed out small packs of stapled paper.

"Welcome everyone," Ian was speaking. "Today we'll be reading sides from Samuel Beckett's Endgame. In doing so, I'll get to know you and your voices and will cast accordingly. No acting, please."

Huh? What did that mean – no acting? Patty handed me the pages with a smile and nostril flare. She knew I was dying on the inside. The first words on the page: Bare Interior and Gray Light. The characters were Hamm and his son Clov, and Hamm's parents who lived in trash cans in the living room – dying. We read along, taking different parts, including the stage directions. Every ten minutes or more Ian would mumble something into Patty's ear, and she'd scribble on the clipboard, nodding her head in agreement or understanding. I had no idea what I was reading and just tried to enunciate well. The play sounded like The Three Stooges, which is what I told Patty on the train heading home during rush hour crowded with businessmen in gray suits and trench coats smoking and reading the Philadelphia Inquirer.

"It is nothing like the Stooges! It's avant-garde. The Stooges are ignoramuses."

"All the characters are old, and the only female character has practically no lines and dies! It makes no sense!"

"That's what avant-garde is!"

"I meant for a girl's school to do a play with all male roles! The play doesn't make sense either. It's depressing."

"So if Ian wants to cast you I should tell him what you said?"

"No! Why would you – does he want to cast me?"

"How would I know?"

"I don't want to be in a trash can. You can tell him that."

"He may not use trash cans. He may have Nagg and Nell in invisible trash cans. The audience could see them so they'd have to be like statues – frozen the whole time, except when they speak. Do you think you could do that?"

"I don't know."

"Because if you move just a miniscule of an inch you'd ruin the whole illusion, and hence, the play." How much time had Patty spent with this guy?

"I just want to do a normal play and play a part of a normal girl like the other schools."

"What, you wanna do Oklahoma or Oliver?"

"I wish."

"Those shows are big fat musicals and O'Hara and St. James have real stages and musical directors and most importantly – money!"

"I know that."

"Besides, why do what everybody else is doing? Samuel Beckett is cutting edge."

"There are plays that aren't musicals that have normal speaking people and parts for girls. We could do Antigone! I already have my costume."

"So you think Ian would give you the lead role?"

"No. I don't know... maybe."

"That's so conceited."

"It's not conceited. It's confident. If anybody's conceited, it's you."

"So? Nothing wrong with being a little conceited once in a while."

Our stop was next. I was hungry and exhausted from trying to keep up with Patty. If we were animals one of us would have eaten the other by now, but we were reasonably healthy baby-boom Catholic girls in pleated plaid skirts and knee socks with a red brick home a half mile away. We'd never be that hungry.

One o'clock the next day, the cast list was still not up. Every chance I had, I went by the glass enclosed bulletin board outside the main office and took discreet passing glances. Ian was sending a mixed message. I started making other plans in my head. I was making friends. Well at least one friend, whose family owned a grocery store in the neighborhood. She asked me what I was doing after school, maybe I'd want to hang out at her house and do Spanish homework together. We could raid the store beforehand for snacks.

Patty delivered the message to me during algebra. Ian had cast me as Clov. First rehearsal was at three-thirty in Mary Martin's room. Patty was at the door, handing out paperbacks of the play as we walked into the room. Antoinette did not look happy. She was cast as Nagg, father of Hamm, who had few lines and died after his one monologue on page fifty-six. Vicki Updike was cast as Hamm. She was close to six feet, had a slight stoop and a strong jaw. She was a senior, as were Antoinette and Maryann Martino, who was cast as Nell, Hamm's mother. These girls exuded confidence and had visible bust lines. They definitely had more life experience than me. Why would anyone give a prepubescent first-time thespian the biggest role in any play, let alone a play that was undecipherable?

Clov was the only character that was upright and mobile throughout the entire play. He never sat down and spent his life pushing his father around in an 'easy chair' on castors. Ian encouraged me to look through my father's closet for costume ideas.

"Why not my brother's?" I asked him. I'd have to wash them first but I actually liked Greg's clothes.

"Too predictable," was his quick reply. Great, not only did I have to translate the play, I'd have to deconstruct everything the man said.

"He's super intelligent. His IQ is off the charts." Patty wouldn't stop talking about Ian or her ideas for the set. It was rush hour again and we were stuck in the smoking car – standing. The 'Endgame world' was following me home. She was also doing her best to ignore the conductor, who wasn't Barry, so he wouldn't notice us and we'd get a free ride, which we would normally get when Barry was on duty. All I could think about were those other girls in Oklahoma and Oliver singing and dancing in gorgeous dresses with bodices and twirling skirts looking beautiful and kissing boys, while I'd be in my father's flannels, scratching my groin, crying: "I have a flea!" Life wasn't fair.

"Why the big puss?" Patty was pulling me deeper into the throng of gray suits.

"I have to scratch myself – down there – in front of everybody!"

"That's going to be so great if you do it right. We can practice. I'll show you."

"I don't need you to show me."

"Then what's the problem?"

"Nothing. Forget it." I turned away from her and smacked my face into an armpit of a gray suit. Perfect. I was already living the part of Clov without even trying.

Rehearsals were going to be every day after school Monday to Thursday and Saturday afternoons. Patty was in charge of making the schedule and noting the pages we would work on. Not only did I have a zillion lines to learn, I had to remember where I said them because Clov was always moving around – for no reason at all!

"You have a big responsibility." It was Friday night and I'd just gotten into bed. I was exhausted after a week of being Clov and had to face him again the next day. Patty was still fully dressed and awake. "Clov is the first person to come onstage. If you blow it, you blow it for the drama club and St. Bernadette's for all time."

"Turn the light off!"

"Did you hear what I said?"

"Shut up!"

"Ian's gonna keep you after rehearsal tomorrow."

"What? Why?" Now I was the one awake.

"You have something better to do?"

"Yeah."

"Like what?" Patty was putting her nightgown on.

I had plans to meet the girl with the grocery store – Gigi – and hang out somewhere where there might be boys. That's all I knew. It wasn't set in stone yet, but I was looking forward to whatever it was we were going to do.

"None of your business. Why does he wanna keep me after?"

"Cause of what I just said. You hafta do a good job with the opening of the play or we'll lose the audience's attention." Patty was now in her bed, suddenly looking sleepy.

"I don't say anything! I just carry a ladder around. Why can't we skip that part and get to the talking? It'll be boring – watching me carry a ladder around." Patty was on her back, eyes closed, slack-jawed. I got out of bed and turned off the light.

The next morning Patty brought me a pair of our dad's corduroy slacks and a flannel shirt.

"Ian wants you to wear these to rehearsal."

"What!?"

"This is what real actors do."

"They're not even washed!"

"Exactly." Patty was wearing her low-cut jeans and a thin muslin peasant blouse with a scoop neck that had a draw string to control the depth of the scoop. "Do you want to be a real actor or not?" She was at the mirror applying liquid liner to her eyes. I was in my underwear – cotton waste high panties and my training bra – which was actually half a sleeveless undershirt more or less. If a stranger walked into the room at that moment, they would definitely think I was the stage manager, and she was the actress.

"First of all – I wanted to be an actress, not an actor –"

"Real actors call themselves actors no matter if they're a man or woman."

"I don't wanna wear dad's stinkin' clothes!"

"Fine! Just bring them with you. I'm meeting Ian for coffee before rehearsal. We're gonna go over the schedule for the day. I'll see you there."

Coffee? Since when did Patty start drinking coffee?

"Oh, and we'll be on the stage in the gym – finally – which'll be so cool." Patty sprayed herself with Patchouli, took one last look in the mirror, and swept out of the room.

My dad gave me a clean shirt and pair of pants and drove me to the school. He adhered to a self-imposed five mile per hour below the speed limit rule.

"Where'd they get this guy?"

"I don't know."

"Sounds like a beatnik."

"He's got a clubfoot."

"Clubfoot wouldn't stop anyone from being a beatnik. Stop him from being sent to Vietnam, but you could still be a beatnik with a clubfoot. Or a hippie. How do you know he has a clubfoot?"

"He can't walk right. He drags his leg."

"Which leg? Right leg?"

"Yea. I think so."

"You're not sure?"

"I don't know." We were coming up to a green light and I could feel the car slowing down, daring it to go yellow and of course it did. I wished I was on the train. I could go over my lines. "What difference does it make?"

"You ever see him barefoot?"

"No. Why?"

"Well... Maybe he's acting like he has a clubfoot."

I never knew if my dad was joking when he came up with these paranoid theories. He had a point. I thought it only polite to avert my eyes from the bottom half of Ian's body. Cars were honking and some drivers were taking their lives into their own hands, passing us on one lane roads.

"You never know... I'd keep my eye on what foot he drags around – these hippie beatniks. I don't trust them. He smoke? Cigarettes?"

"Yea. You're going too slow!" He applied a tiny more pressure to the gas with a slight smile.

"What brand?"

"They're brown. I think they're foreign."

"Get a look at the pack when you can. Jot down that brand name. Something fishy is going on here."

"Nothing fishy, he's just making us do a weirdo play. Dad, can you go a little faster? I'm gonna be late."

"You in a hurry to put on my clothes and do this weirdo play?" He was looking straight at me with his foot on the gas. "I can go faster." My dad was making no sense. He was acting like Hamm. Endgame was haunting me.

Patty's peasant blouse was scooped to its lowest depth, revealing the slight hollow between her breasts and a little lace. She was reading the schedule for the day from her clip board, checking off the tasks as she read them. We were going to start with the Nagg and Nell scene so Antoinette and Maryann could leave early. We would then 'work through' Hamm and Clov's opening scene and then Vicki could leave. Afterwards Ian could work with me on the opening scene where I ran around like an idiot with a ladder and said a bunch of lines that made no sense.

Antoinette and Maryann were hysterical in their scene. I had no idea what they were saying, but it didn't matter, they were entertaining and had the rest of us in stitches.

I was jealous of their success in pleasing Ian and Patty. There was no way I could bring a similar pleasure to anyone with my performance. Maryann and Antoinette were giving me the snub or maybe I was imagining it – I wasn't sure if I was projecting these feelings after experiencing my father's suspicion. But from their point of view, I could see the collapse of St. Bernadette's drama club with my abysmal portrayal of one of the most beloved characters of the avant-garde. But they were the ones that gave Ian the job! Why didn't they just – End. This. Game? Wow. I was becoming avant-garde to myself!

Ian was treading back and forth in front of the stage, dragging his right leg, stroking his beard with his left hand and smoking with the other. He'd decided that we'd just work on my opening lines – save the 'ladder mime' for later in the week. My homework was to come up with Clov's 'objective' for moving the ladder and what caused me to laugh. That was another thing – I had to laugh several times in that ladder bit. Why couldn't I cry? That I could do.

I'd already gone through my lines three times and he still wasn't happy. The fourth time I was giving it as much feeling as possible – incorporating hand gestures and fluctuating my voice.

"...Grain upon grain, one by one, and one day, suddenly, there's a heap, a little heap, the impossible heap. (pause, as I shook my head woefully). I can't be punished anymore." (pause, as I turned upstage).

I was just about to say my next line when Ian interrupted me.

"What are you doing?"

"Acting?" I hoped to God that was the answer he was looking for. I was never quite sure. A rose was not always a rose in Ian's world – it was sometimes a capitalistic ploy.

"Well stop it!" He took a deep angry drag off his brown cigarette. Brand name – I have to remember to get the brand name for my dad. An exhale of smoke escaped from both nostrils.

"I am waiting for you to tell me about this impossible heap. What is it?" I looked over at Patty for a clue. She was absorbed in blowing bubbles and examining her hair for split ends. That hurt. She was certainly focused when the other actors were doing the talking. Ian was waiting for an answer.

"I'm not sure... sand?"

"You think the greatest dramatic poet of the twentieth century would muse on a pile of sand?"

"I don't know – maybe." Oh no, what did I do? It looked like a cloud of doom had come to rest on Ian's shoulders.

"Have you even read your script?"

"Yes!" How dare he! Novice that I was, I knew that was the worst accusation one thespian could lay on another.

"You think, like the masses, that Samuel Beckett is just a dispenser of meaningless gloom?" Now he was just being mean. After two weeks in Clov's musty world, I fully understood that gloom was something to be treasured, given out stringently – not dispensed!

"I just don't understand what this guy is saying." There. I said it. The truth, no matter how scary, was out. That got Patty's attention.

"But you must! It is your job as an actor to get into his soul, to understand the origin of every utterance." Ian's stature was shrinking, his knees were caving, along with an over earnest upper body, he looked as if he was proposing marriage, or pleading for his life.

"Well, how do I do that?" I really wanted to please him.

"You must live the part! You must eat, drink, sleep, and defecate as Clov."

I was going to pretend he never said that last part. Even Patty looked stunned.

"But he never sits down!"

"Then, to be a true actor, to be true to your character – you must not sit down."

I did not expect acting to be like this. At fourteen I was beginning to, to quote Clov, "…see my light dying."

The next day I stood through all of my classes. That afternoon, the principal, Sister Elizabeth, sat in on a rehearsal. The next day Ian was not in Mary Martin's room, nor was Patty. But Miss Findlay was and told us that we were not going to be doing Endgame. We were going to do Our Town, an American play by Thornton Wilder. It had a big cast and all of the drama club members would have a part.

Miss Findlay cast me in the role of Emily, a young woman who spoke like a normal person and sat down. However, Emily died in childbirth, but unlike Nell, who went further into the trash can and closed the lid when she died, Emily lived on after death. I wore a red gingham dress in life and a silky white gown in death. Vicki played George, my husband, and Antoinette was cast in the main role – the Stage Manager. Patty had decided that theater was not her thing and signed up for a Driver's Ed class. No one ever heard from Ian again. I never got the name of his cigarette brand nor was I absolutely certain which foot was clubbed, nor was Patty. I didn't have the nerve to ask any of the other girls.

There were three performances, all a big success. At our last show, Patty brought me a bouquet of roses during the curtain call. I didn't even know she was in the audience. She'd passed her driver's test that day and had driven herself and Greg to the play.

"This is my little sister!" She was telling and reminding everybody and anybody during the after-show party. "That was my sister on that stage!"

Later that night in our room she said, "I was afraid to see the show 'cause I didn't think you could act. But then I thought that maybe that other part wasn't right for you. But you were sooooo good in this part! It didn't look like you were acting. How'd ya do that? And real tears! You gotta teach me how to act."

I knew she'd forget she said that last sentence by the next morning. She'd be on to the next project. It didn't matter to me. Life was too precious, too precious to worry about Patty. I needed to realize life while I lived it. It was too late for Emily, but not for me.

My First Kiss

It was a sultry August evening in rural Pennsylvania. I was sitting in the back seat of a shiny green Volkswagen bug, next to a boy named 'Rick'. He was a lanky, blonde boy with sleepy blue eyes and a short pouty mouth. I was fourteen and still hadn't started menstruating, so I smoked. I smoked because I was stressed over the whole puberty business. It had too much control over my life and that pissed me off. I smoked because I still looked nine years old and needed to disarm the jerks that were quick to treat me as such. And I smoked because I was desperately trying to fit in somewhere… and semi-delinquency seemed the most accessible path for me.

My cousin Gretchen was in the front seat, with her big breasts and perfect nose, next to an older dark-haired boy who was driving. These were her friends. This was her territory. She didn't really want me to come but her mother made her take me so the adults could drink in peace. I was just along for the ride, and I had to make a good impression or at least not screw up anymore than I had earlier that night. Gretchen had whispered to me, with solemnity, that she had her 'friend'. "Where is she?" I asked. My cousin fell back on her bed, kicking and screaming in laughter, then jumped up, ran out of the room and down the stairs into the living room, and announced to our parents and another severe looking couple, what I had said.

My mother made my cousin promise to 'put it out of her mind!' and not to mention it to her 'other' friends. Both she and Gretchen got a laugh out of that but choked it back when they saw my face which was in a big 'puss'. Gretchen, with her high cheekbones and spotless skin, looked more like my mother's daughter than I did. I knew the two of them thought as much, with the secret smug smiles they gave to each other when they 'accidently' found themselves in front of a mirror. For a few seconds I imagined the car crashing and everyone surviving except me. What then? Would my mother want to slap Gretchen or adopt her? That would be an interesting test.

Gretchen's dad, my Uncle George, was my mother's brother. He looked like Clark Gable. On a Christmas visit when I was eleven, I walked in on him sitting on the toilet. It was a humiliation I tried desperately to live down. In my mind when these people saw me, they saw a toilet trespasser, a bathroom barger – a nuisance. So, every time we visited, I tried to reinvent myself. This outing would be a test. The older you got, the more tests there were, it seemed.

From the snippets of conversation I caught over the sputtering and grinding of the car, they were looking for someone for some reason; but if they found someone else that would be okay too and then we would get out of the car.

"Cool," I offered to no one in particular, on my own accord, as I exhaled a haboob of smoke into the back of the driver's head. As in response or solidarity to my remark, or for the sake of comfort, Rick stretched his left arm along the back of the seat, brushing my head in the effort. It felt like my heart was going to smash through my chest and gash a hole in my peasant blouse. I discreetly ran my fingers through my hair on both sides in an attempt to hide my burning red face.

This was the first time I was in a car with a driver under thirty, but more importantly the first time I was in such close proximity to a boy other than my brothers since I was eleven and looked like one myself. I was a Catholic school girl. The Philadelphia Archdiocese had separated the boys and girls in the seventh and eighth grades, and in a couple of weeks, I would be returning to St. Bernadette's, an all-girls private academy, for my sophomore year. I let myself relax back into the seat, brushing my head against Rick's wrist and wished the night would go on forever.

Gretchen poked her head around her seat and announced, "We can only hang out for two hours. Her mother wants her back at 9:30."

What was my cousin doing to me? I tried to object, "I don't hafta – ", but the bitch cut me off.

"Yes, you do. Your mother would kill you and then she'd kill me." She turned her head in Rick's direction and said with salaciousness, "Her mother is scary strict."

What a two-face! I exhaled an airstream of tobacco directly onto her face to make her turn around and stop interfering with the natural chain of events that the universe intended to happen in that back seat at that time between me and a boy named Rick. Instead, she retaliated with a gust of Pall Mall in my direction. "Does she know you're a chain smoker?" She asked before taking another drag from her cigarette.

"No." I answered.

"She will after tonight."

"Only if you tell her." I tossed my cigarette out the window then pulled a roll of mint life savers from my denim cut-offs and popped a few into my mouth. Gretchen stuck her hand in my face.

"It's bad manners not to offer first."

I pulled a candy from the roll and dropped it in her hand without bothering to peel a scrap of foil off it.

"What if they were poisoned?" I asked in my spookiest voice.

"Very funny!" She said sarcastically as she turned around.

This scene got a soft chuckle out of Rick. I think he likes me, I thought, as I placed a foil free mint in his open palm.

"Thanks." He said.

"Welcome," I replied.

"Wintergreen?" He asked.

"Yeah!" I answered. In too loud a voice.

We rode in silence for the next thirty seconds, sucking on our mints. There was some fiddling and fussing with the radio in the front seat. After another thirty seconds, 'In-A-Gadda-Da-Vida' came blasting from the radio. The driver said something to Rick via the rear-view mirror. Rick response was something like "Yeaaa!" I felt his body moving in sync with the electric guitar, his free hand drumming on his long thin thigh while his left hand rhythmically rubbed my neck and scalp. Happiness abounded in the car.

"Butterfly." Rick said.

"They're so cool." I offered.

"Far out." He responded.

At that moment, I thought, as the car skidded and sped on the dark winding roads of Pottsville, I might die tonight and that would be okay just as long as I was kissed before the car smashed into smithereens.

Our first stop was a 7 Eleven parking lot. My cousin and the driver stuck their heads out their respective windows and held conversations with leather and suede skinny figures, whose faces were not visible until one surrounded in brown hair squeezed into Gretchen's window and gave a nod to the back seat. I took a drag off my cigarette with

189

indifference as did Rick. The driver was handed a bottle wrapped in a brown paper bag. He took a swig from it then handed it to Gretchen who took an even bigger swig. She passed it back to the driver who looked into the rear-view mirror and held the bottle up as in an offering to the back seat. Rick grumbled something that sounded like "no" while Gretchen giggled something admonishing which I was sure had to do with me and my mother and our horrible relationship which I was now learning was 'hilarious' to her.

The driver took another swig then handed it over to whoever gave it to him. That face appeared in the window and said something to Rick, who was not interested. There was some chuckling between the driver and his friend, and Gretchen and her friend, before we went whizzing out of the parking lot, slamming into the curb and onto the road.

So, I thought to myself, this is what public school kids did. They drove around listening to the radio while hopping from bowling alley parking lots to 7 Elevens looking for action. Cool! I was frequently grounded and stayed in my room listening to Leonard Cohen and writing dark odes about my mother.

For the next hour I wasn't sure where we were or what was happening anywhere outside the realm of the back seat. When I felt Rick's fingers were tangled in my hair, I pretended not to notice by becoming motionless, leaving it up to him to decide if his fingers found themselves entwined in my tresses accidentally or on purpose. Meanwhile my inside voice was acting like an idiot and screaming: "Yes! Yes! Touch it! Touch it more!"

As if in response to my mind, Gretchen turned around, looked at the two of us and cooed, "Don't you two look cozy!"

Turn around you nasty bitch, I wanted to say. I hated her. So self-confident and grown up in the front seat in her Playtex bra and pancake make-up, breaking the mood in my back seat. I pulled out another

190

cigarette. Rick flicked a match with his right hand and lit my cig and his with one light. I loved him! Sure, we'd barely spoken since we were introduced, but I was positive we were communicating on some kind of deep tobacco induced plane reserved for all those lonely teenagers relegated to the back seat of tiny cars. Two outcasts, I thought, maybe existentialists? We smoked in silence as our thighs touched and I yearned to be kissed. I thought that a kiss from a real boy would be like a magic spell and set everything in motion. My breasts would sprout, I'd get my period and be out of the puberty hell I'd been trapped in for over three years, and on my way to becoming a woman.

"It's 9:15!" Gretchen's squeal broke my profound thoughts and sent Rick's fingers directly onto my shoulder. "Oh no!" My brain screamed. I had heard how boys could tell if you were wearing a bra by feeling for the straps. My straps were cottony thick. I was wearing a training bra. According to my mother, I needed some sort of initiation into the real, satiny, lacy world of cups, straps, hooks, and eyes necessary to safely encase one's mammary glands. My mammary glands were barely noticeable. The driver stopped short at a red light; I fell into Rick's lap as his hand slid down onto my upper arm. We were in some kind of stiff half-embrace. I lifted my head off his chest out of courtesy. It seemed too intimate.

"You comfortable?" He asked.

"Yeah!" I blurted, although I was incredibly physically uncomfortable, but it was worth the pain to be in his arm. It was a long red light. For the first time since we stopped, I looked at the front seat. Gretchen and the dark-haired boy were kissing – more like swallowing each other's face. It looked painful and unsanitary. Where was I supposed to put my eyes? Gretchen's blouse was unbuttoned, and his hands were all over, tugging at that big, padded bra. The light turned green, but they kept sucking and gnawing at each other, like two puppies in a cage. Horns started honking, but the two kept on until Rick smacked the dark-haired boy in the head.

"Dave!" He shouted. Dave and Gretchen unwound themselves from each other and the car puttered into the intersection as the light turned yellow. Before Dave could get the car back into gear and zoom forward, it turned red, leaving the line of angry cars behind him.

Once the car started moving, Rick's arm tightened around my shoulders. Out of the corner of my eye I could see his head turn toward me. I felt his eyes watching, waiting. For the first time in two hours, I fully turned my neck and looked up at his full huge face as it started coming down onto mine. I had no idea what I was supposed to do, so I instinctively tilted my chin up and closed my eyes like Scarlet O'Hara did when she gave herself to Rhett Butler. But then I started thinking about my Uncle George, so I squeezed my eyes tighter to make my mind shut up, and then I felt it – a spark! Our lips had touched. His felt cushy and a little chafed. Now what? I'd come this far, but I had no instructions! I decided to just follow his lead. His lips pressed into mine, I pressed back. He cocked his head to the right and I cocked mine to the left... our noses smashed so I changed direction. So, we just pressed and cocked and pressed and cocked, over the bumps and gravel, until the car came to a complete stop, and we were thrown against each other, and rebounded into the doors.

Rick held the door open for me as I climbed out from the back seat. He had a smile on his face that made me feel ashamed and excited at the same time. We said goodnight, and he hopped into the front seat and the green bug crawled away. I looked over at my cousin, who was buttoning up her blouse.

"So, did you have fun?" She asked.

"I guess," I said.

"Do I look okay?"

The bottom half of her face was smeared in pink lipstick; the mascara and eye shadow had smudged together and formed zombie circles around her eyes. There was a sprinkle of ashes in her hair.

"Take a picture it'll last longer."

Her buttons were off track.

"You look good."

"Can I have one of those mints?" She held out her hand.

I unraveled the foil before I placed it in her palm. I didn't tell her that it was my last mint and I was saving it for myself. She needed it more than I did.

Epilogue – February 2001

Treading Deep Waters

It was a Tuesday, the night before our father's funeral when my sister Patty told me about my birth. How tiny I was, how our mother was so miserable carrying me.

The last time I had seen my sister was March 1999, almost two years before, when she visited me in New York for a couple of days. We had stayed in touch, more or less since then, and for the past two weeks our relationship had built up some steam as I kept her abreast of our father's condition – Mesothelioma. She had been hoping to be taken up on her offer to be his hospice nurse, but our mother was uncomfortable with that idea. She and Patty had had one of their infamous fallouts in May 1999 after my sister had shown up late for our younger brother's wedding with a Jamaican orderly who worked at her hospital. The man was wearing a Rasta Tam under which was a mound of dreads that he uncovered before walking into the reception.

It wasn't so much that he was Jamaican, or that he had dreadlocks down to his waist; it was because he and Patty stole the show. Not only

194

did the two rip up the dance floor, but he, Javel, was so charming and enticing, he had all the women over 70 on their feet, including my brother's spanking new mother-in-law and our own mother. However, the newlyweds and our father, were not so easily charmed. Therefore, our mother had a bit of public 'day after' regrets for falling under the spell of a younger exotic man, and also for exposing her uninhibited prowess on the dance floor to the likes that no one, including her husband, had ever seen. She had lost control and blamed it on Patty rather than the half dozen flutes of champagne that she had downed on an empty stomach.

We were in the living-room, in the house where we grew up, sitting on the floor in front of an antique French Maple cabinet, drinking chamomile tea. The cabinet had two doors and initially housed our family's first television, a fifties' black and white. Now an antique bowl and pitcher rested atop it, the doors stayed closed. This cabinet used to appear in my dreams as the Confessional. Both had a similar blonde wood, only this wood looked like it was mixed with butterscotch. Those dreams were no longer in my memory bank, but I had a strong sense they'd be making a comeback after this visit. Our parents had continued to live in this house long after the four of us had left. For the past two days, Patty and I had been staying with our mother, who was upstairs having her shower, and we would be staying another two nights. Our brothers lived in the area, so they were free to come and go, escaping to their own homes.

"Why are you telling me this now?"

"I thought it was time you knew. And since he's gone, she'll have little defense when you confront her." Patty gave a heavy sigh of importance and gulped her tea. The string from the tea bag clung to the side of her mug. She was wearing purple contacts and had hennaed her short thick hair into a near matching shade. In two weeks, she would turn forty-eight.

"I'm not going to confront her –"

"Not today, but sometime soon you'll want to. Trust me. There's more to this."

"What more can there be? I know I was six weeks early and four pounds, so what?"

"I just told you! She was miserable and induced the labor."

"You didn't tell me that! How could she induce the labor?"

My sister pushed herself off the floor with one hand as she held her mug in the other.

"Why are we sitting on the floor like dogs?" She stepped to the other side of the room and plopped herself in the middle of the couch.

"Come join me."

I was glad she was on the other side of the room. I needed a buffer zone lest I fall under the spell of her purple eyes. I rested my back against the cabinet and stretched out my legs. This position felt good.

"Tell me how she induced her labor."

"She didn't so much induce as she caused it with her cigarette smoking, the four miscarriages she had before you, her depression, and she was on drugs. They had to yank you out with the forceps."

"How do you know all this? You were four!"

"Look at this picture!" Patty pulled a picture from her fanny pack which she had been wearing since she arrived. It was a 4x4 black & white with scalloped edges. The picture was a profile view of my mother sitting in a rocker wearing a black and white organdy dress under a full apron, holding infant me. I'm looking at the camera, and she is staring straight ahead. Her hair is a short pixie cut; her lips are full and painted. Her face looks chiseled with its high cheekbones, and strong, feminine jaw line. She's holding me like she would a bundle of laundry or a bag of groceries it seems.

"You see how skinny she is here! You were maybe... two months? She was on diet pills!"

I thought that I had seen every photo ever taken of me. Our father was a bit of a shutter bug. But I'd never seen this one.

"Why do you have this picture?"

"I was trying to protect you."

"From what?"

"Getting hurt. This photograph shows her indifference to you."

"And now you're trying to hurt me! What proof do you have she was taking pills?"

"Because she told me."

Our mother allowed my sister only one visit with our father during his illness – on New Year's Day. She'd finally given her the green light to come to his bedside on Sunday. Patty immediately charged across the state in her orange Toyota only to pull up in front of the house as our father was exiting in a body bag. My sister wanted revenge. This was how she was doing it, as always, through me.

"Confront her? And then what? Have you ever done that?"

"Of course, I have!"

"When?"

"All the time. I don't put up with her... you know, her stuff."

It was somewhat true. Patty avoided her or took the punishment, but she had survived. She was stronger than me. But I didn't understand why she was feeding me this crap and why now?

"Cassie, look at me."

I didn't realize I wasn't. I was still focused on the picture, how sad my mother looked, how stupid and not cute I did.

"Oh Cassie, I don't mean to sound mean, but you haven't really –"

Oh no. I hadn't the strength to brace myself for another hurt. Patty had not seen our father writhing in agony. The sad irony was that she was the most qualified person in the family who could have taken charge of the situation, administered the stronger dose of pain medication, which our mother was too afraid to do. I was still reeling from those scenes.

"Cassie, I tried to protect you. You didn't have all your parts when you were born – I mean yeah – physically you're really strong. But mentally? Remember all the trouble you had in school? That's why I encouraged you to draw and paint and act. Remember what she said about you if you didn't go to St. Bernadette's and went to the public school, where they'd put you?"

"Basket Weaving."

"She knew. Cassie, honey – you're not so smart. But you've got a sixth sense. You see things under and beneath the surface. You just miss the real-world stuff. I knew you were struggling with school and every time I tried to help you, she made me get out of the room. Remember?"

I could feel my heart shattering into slivers of glass. She had tapped life into one of those memories that I'd let die because I was never sure if they were real or I had embellished them – our mother squashing me, preventing me from developing. "No," was her favorite word when it came to any 'ask' from me. "It's easier to say 'yes,'" was her refrain when she denied me any fun. I first had to get better grades. Yet she never helped me.

Patty had joined me on the floor. She was too close. "I kinda wished she'd gone first," she whispered in my ear.

I didn't. I had always assumed that my mother and I would become closer once my father was gone. I thought we had a deep-rooted, hidden bond. She told me – several times – that the next-door neighbor yelled at her when she came home from the hospital after giving birth to Freddy. "That little girl sat on that step for three days waiting for you while you went and had another baby! You have enough children!"

That story inspired the 'bond' belief. But as I replayed the scene in my mind while listening to my sister, another layer began to unpeel. I did remember sitting on the front step waiting for her every day for three days, all day. I was three. I can picture the sun shining on the steps, and the stones and chips beneath the cement sparkling. I might have brought out a doll or a tea set, something to play with. I was terrified she was gone forever but hadn't tapped into that fear. I was filling the space with babbling and activity, all alone. I had a visceral belief that the sun rose and set under my mother's direction; that she required a kind of worship and that my sitting and waiting on the step would ensure her return. Once she was home and settled, I'd sit outside her bedroom when she took her nap, protecting, guarding.

This was the relationship that prevailed through my forty-four years. She was the one I answered to, apologized to, who I always wanted to please, and later in life vehemently rebelled against. This dysfunction transferred to every woman I came across in life who was in a position of authority – a teacher, employer, director. I feared, revered, and cowered to them. Not men. I got around men with my sexuality. I had no idea it was there, inside, working me. It was a force of its own.

"You couldn't think for yourself." Patty was still talking.

"I get it, Patty! Why didn't you do anything then? Why didn't you tell me this, years – decades ago? Why are you so concerned now? What do you want?"

It didn't matter if Patty was telling the truth or bullshitting. The essence of her message was clear and resounded within me. It'd been there, buried deep inside my tissues, like a cancer. I thought of my dad and felt a pang in my chest.

"So, this is what we're gonna do. In two weeks, we're going to confront her. We'll take her to lunch, she loves going to lunch, and talk to her. We'll tell her you deserve some compensation for your life. How hard you've worked and have so little. Because she's gonna get a lot of money from Dad's settlement –"

We hear the bathroom door open and our mother's flat-footed stomping into her bedroom. A steamy gust of dial soap and menthol drift down into the parlor. There is an urgency to my mother's movements and then a weak, frightened wail, "Paaaatttyyyy!"

My sister and I look at each other in alarm.

We scurried up the two-tiered, nine step carpeted staircase into the first bedroom on the right, the room we shared for eight years. Our mother was sitting in the rocking chair – the same chair in the photo – one leg on the ottoman with a wad of scrunched toilet paper in the center of her skinny calf. She was wearing a pale pink cotton silk nightgown and robe ensemble.

"Mom! You shaved your legs?" Patty was on her knees between the ottoman and the chair.

"I feel so stupid." Our mother was covering her face with one hand, stifling a sob. The toilet tissue was now soaked in blood. I grabbed a box of tissues from her night table and handed it to Patty.

"Mom, you don't have any hair on your legs," I said, with a slight chuckle, trying to soften the scene.

My sister was carefully removing the toilet tissue, her other hand at the ready with a thick orderly square of Kleenex. As soon as she lifted the tissue, a geyser of thick red-black blood gushed from the leg before her other hand closed in on the wound. She'd cut one of her varicose veins. My mother gasped and grabbed Patty's wrist.

"Your father would kill me if I don't show up tomorrow." My mother – always joking at the worst of moments. This was one of the traits that I inherited and admired; however, there were other qualities we shared that I found less attractive – her impatience, hyper-criticalness, jealousy, and bitterness. But I couldn't think about those now because she was bleeding – profusely. I rushed to the bathroom and yanked the roll of toilet paper from the wall and hurried back into the room to see my sister sitting on the edge of the rocker, her face buried in my mother's chest, my mother's arms tight around her. I look at my mother, expecting her to see me, but her eyes are closed, tears trickling down her cheeks, her lips trembling. The tissue on the leg was holding on its own, looking like a fully bloomed red rose.

"Mom?" I say, half-heartedly, not sure if I wanted a response.

The chair seemed to be rocking itself, perhaps by the beating of two hearts together with me, once again, on the outside looking in. Could they have rocked that chair together if not for me? I wondered.

Terri is a New York based writer/actor/educator. Her award-winning solo show, "Following the Yellow Brick Road Down the Rabbit Hole," an exploration of the Catholic church and sexuality, was inspired by the early stories in "Our Lady of Perpetual Sorrow." Her prose has been published by Washington Square Review; Inkwell Journal and Cafe Lit. Her plays have been staged and produced at venues in the New York/New Jersey area including Women Center Stage, Emerging Artists, New Georges, New Jersey Rep. Her monologues have been published with Meriwether and Smith & Kraus. This is her first novel, and she is currently working on a screen play of the book.

Acknowledgements

I am eternally grateful to Donna Miele for her insight and generosity, without whose encouragement I would have continued the unending struggle to transform these stories into a traditional novel form.

A huge thank you to Coree Spencer who introduced me to Charles Salzberg and the Writer's Workshop – a gift that keeps on giving. I am so appreciative to these two kindhearted and talented people, and to my fellow classmates, Wendy Davis, Cynthia Ehrenkrantz, Phyllis Melhado, Andy Zimmerman, Jack Epler, Judy Rabnor, Karen Gershowitz, Liz Ectingley, and Carol Horowitz, for their perceptive feedback.

I am much obliged to the Wainwright House and Manhattanville College for hosting Writing workshops with Maureen Amaruto and Donna Miele.

To my long-time friends and colleagues – Stuart D'Ver, Cynthia Hanson and Kathryn Paulsen, thank you for your continual support.

Thank you to Willow River Press for taking on this project and launching it into the world.

Printed in the USA
CPSIA information can be obtained
at www.ICGtesting.com
LVHW031951110424
777140LV00012B/325

9 781958 901700